Curriculum Units

GRADE

2

Pockets, Teeth, and Favorite Things

Data Analysis

UNIT **4**

Complicated Kris Northern

"This image illustrates some of the best qualities of fractals—infinity, reiteration, and self similarity."– **Kris Northern**

Investigations
IN NUMBER, DATA, AND SPACE®

Glenview, Illinois • Boston, Massachusetts
Chandler, Arizona • Upper Saddle River, New Jersey

The Investigations curriculum was developed by TERC, Cambridge, MA.

This material is based on work supported by the National Science Foundation ("NSF") under Grant No. ESI-0095450. Any opinions, findings, and conclusions or recommendations expressed in this material are those of the author(s) and do not necessarily reflect the views of the National Science Foundation.

ISBN-13: 978-0-328-60014-4

ISBN-10: 0-328-60014-8

4 5 6 7 8 9 10 V064 16 15 14 13 12

T E R C

Co-Principal Investigators

Susan Jo Russell

Karen Economopoulos

Authors

Lucy Wittenberg
Director Grades 3–5

Karen Economopoulos
Director Grades K–2

Virginia Bastable
(SummerMath for Teachers,
Mt. Holyoke College)

Katie Hickey Bloomfield

Keith Cochran

Darrell Earnest

Arusha Hollister

Nancy Horowitz

Erin Leidl

Megan Murray

Young Oh

Beth W. Perry

Susan Jo Russell

Deborah Schifter
(Education
Development Center)

Kathy Sillman

Administrative Staff

Amy Taber
Project Manager

Beth Bergeron

Lorraine Brooks

Emi Fujiwara

Contributing Authors

Denise Baumann

Jennifer DiBrienza

Hollee Freeman

Paula Hooper

Jan Mokros

Stephen Monk
(University of Washington)

Mary Beth O'Connor

Judy Storeygard

Cornelia Tierney

Elizabeth Van Cleef

Carol Wright

Technology

Jim Hammerman

Classroom Field Work

Amy Appell

Rachel E. Davis

Traci Higgins

Julia Thompson

Collaborating Teachers

This group of dedicated teachers carried out extensive field testing in their classrooms, met regularly to discuss issues of teaching and learning mathematics, provided feedback to staff, welcomed staff into their classrooms to document students' work, and contributed both suggestions and written material that has been incorporated into the curriculum.

Bethany Altchek

Linda Amaral

Kimberly Beauregard

Barbara Bernard

Nancy Buell

Rose Christiansen

Chris Colbath-Hess

Lisette Colon

Kim Cook

Frances Cooper

Kathleen Drew

Rebeka Eston Salemi

Thomas Fisher

Michael Flynn

Holly Ghazey

Susan Gillis

Danielle Harrington

Elaine Herzog

Francine Hiller

Kirsten Lee Howard

Liliana Klass

Leslie Kramer

Melissa Lee Andrichak

Kelley Lee Sadowski

Jennifer Levitan

Mary Lou LoVecchio

Kristen McEnaney

Maura McGrail

Kathe Millett

Florence Molyneaux

Amy Monkiewicz

Elizabeth Monopoli

Carol Murray

Robyn Musser

Christine Norrman

Deborah O'Brien

Timothy O'Connor

Anne Marie O'Reilly

Mark Paige

Margaret Riddle

Karen Schweitzer

Elisabeth Seyferth

Susan Smith

Debra Sorvillo

Shoshanah Starr

Janice Szymaszek

Karen Tobin

JoAnn Trauschke

Ana Vaisenstein

Yvonne Watson

Michelle Woods

Mary Wright

Note: Unless otherwise noted, all contributors listed above were staff of the Education Research Collaborative at TERC during their work on the curriculum. Other affiliations during the time of development are listed.

Advisors

Deborah Lowenberg Ball,
University of Michigan

Hyman Bass, Professor of Mathematics and Mathematics Education
University of Michigan

Mary Canner, Principal, Natick Public Schools

Thomas Carpenter, Professor of Curriculum and Instruction,
University of Wisconsin-Madison

Janis Freckmann, Elementary Mathematics Coordinator,
Milwaukee Public Schools

Lynne Godfrey, Mathematics Coach,
Cambridge Public Schools

Ginger Hanlon, Instructional Specialist in Mathematics,
New York City Public Schools

DeAnn Huinker, Director, Center for Mathematics and
Science Education Research, University of Wisconsin-Milwaukee

James Kaput, Professor of Mathematics, University of
Massachusetts-Dartmouth

Kate Kline, Associate Professor, Department of Mathematics
and Statistics, Western Michigan University

Jim Lewis, Professor of Mathematics,
University of Nebraska-Lincoln

William McCallum, Professor of Mathematics,
University of Arizona

Harriet Pollatsek, Professor of Mathematics,
Mount Holyoke College

Debra Shein-Gerson, Elementary Mathematics Specialist,
Weston Public Schools

Gary Shevell, Assistant Principal,
New York City Public Schools

Liz Sweeney, Elementary Math Department,
Boston Public Schools

Lucy West, Consultant, Metamorphosis:
Teaching Learning Communities, Inc.

This revision of the curriculum was built on the work of the many authors who contributed to the first edition (published between 1994 and 1998). We acknowledge the critical contributions of these authors in developing the content and pedagogy of *Investigations*:

Authors

Joan Akers

Michael T. Battista

Douglas H. Clements

Karen Economopoulos

Marlene Kliman

Jan Mokros

Megan Murray

Ricardo Nemirovsky

Andee Rubin

Susan Jo Russell

Cornelia Tierney

Contributing Authors

Mary Berle-Carman

Rebecca B. Corwin

Rebeka Eston

Claryce Evans

Anne Goodrow

Cliff Konold

Chris Mainhart

Sue McMillen

Jerrie Moffet

Tracy Noble

Kim O'Neil

Mark Ogonowski

Julie Sarama

Amy Shulman Weinberg

Margie Singer

Virginia Woolley

Tracey Wright

Unit 4

Pockets, Teeth, and Favorite Things

Common Core

Mathematical Practices (MP)

Domains
- Operations and Algebraic Thinking (OA)
- Number and Operations in Base Ten (NBT)
- Measurement and Data (MD)
- Geometry (G)

INVESTIGATION 1
Working with Categorical Data

Day	Session		Common Core Adaptation	Common Core Standards
1	**1.1**	Guess My Rule with People ③ SESSION FOLLOW-UP **Daily Practice and Homework**	**Family Letter:** Make and send home copies of C34–C35, Family Letter, as a replacement for M1–M2, Family Letter.	MP1, MP2, MP4 2.OA.2, 2.NBT.5
2	**1.2**	Guess My Rule with Yekttis		MP1, MP2, MP3 2.NBT.2, 2.NBT.5, 2.G.1
3	**1.3A**	Guess My Rule with Two Rules	See p. CC28.	MP2, MP3, MP4 2.MD.7, 2.G.1
	1.3	Guess My Rule with Two Rules	Skip this session.	
4	**1.4A**	Bar Graphs	See p. CC35.	MP5, MP7 2.OA.2, 2.MD.10
	1.4	"Favorite Things"	Skip this session.	
	1.5	Organizing "Favorite Things" Data	Skip this session.	
	1.6	Sharing "Favorite Things" Data	Skip this session.	
5	**1.7**	Assessment: Favorite Foods and Plus 10 Combinations		MP4 2.NBT.5, 2.MD.10

Pocket and Teeth Data

Day		Session	Common Core Adaptation	Common Core Standards
6	**2.1**	Pocket Towers ④ SESSION FOLLOW-UP Daily Practice	**Homework:** Students sort and represent animal data using *Student Activity Book* pages 18A–18B or C41–C42 (Sorting and Representing Data).	MP2 2.OA.2, 2.NBT.2
7	**2.2**	Pocket Data Representations		MP3 2.OA.2, 2.MD.7
8	**2.3**	How Many Teeth Have You Lost?		MP2 2.NBT.5, 2.MD.10
9	**2.4**	Collecting Teeth Data From Other Classes		MP2 2.NBT.2, 2.MD.8
10	**2.5**	Representing Teeth Data From Other Classes		MP3 2.MD.7, 2.MD.10
11	**2.6**	Comparing Teeth Data		MP2 2.NBT.5, 2.MD.8, 2.MD.10
12	**2.7**	Mystery Teeth Data		MP2, MP7 2.NBT.5, 2.MD.8
13	**2.8**	End-of-Unit Assessment ② ASSESSMENT ACTIVITY End-of-Unit Assessment ④ SESSION FOLLOW-UP Daily Practice	As part of the End-of-Unit Assessment, include C43 to assess the subtraction facts related to near doubles combinations. You may want to give this part of the assessment to 5–6 students at a time so that you can observe how fluently they are able to complete this assessment sheet and then record the information on C44, Assessment Checklist. **Daily Practice:** In addition to *Student Activity Book* page 34, students complete *Student Activity Book* page 35 or C45 (What Do You Collect?) for reinforcement of this unit's content.	MP2, MP3 2.MD.7

Contents

UNIT 4

Pockets, Teeth, and Favorite Things

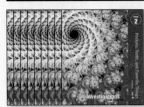

Overview of Program Components

FOR TEACHERS

The **Curriculum Units** are the teaching guides. (See far right.)

Implementing Investigations in Grade 2 offers suggestions for implementing the curriculum. It also contains a comprehensive index.

The **Differentiation and Intervention Guide** offers additional activities for each Investigation to support the range of learners.

Investigations for the Interactive Whiteboard provides whole-class instructional support to enhance each session.

The **Resource Masters and Transparencies CD** contains all reproducible materials that support instruction. The **Shapes CD** provides an environment in which students investigate a variety of geometric ideas.

FOR STUDENTS

The **Student Activity Book** contains the consumable student pages (Recording Sheets, Homework, Practice, and so on).

The **Student Math Handbook** contains Math Words and Ideas pages and Games directions.

The *Investigations* Curriculum

Investigations in Number, Data, and Space® is a K–5 mathematics curriculum designed to engage students in making sense of mathematical ideas. Six major goals guided the development of the *Investigations in Number, Data, and Space*® curriculum. The curriculum is designed to:

- Support students to make sense of mathematics and learn that they can be mathematical thinkers

- Focus on computational fluency with whole numbers as a major goal of the elementary grades

- Provide substantive work in important areas of mathematics—rational numbers, geometry, measurement, data, and early algebra—and connections among them

- Emphasize reasoning about mathematical ideas

- Communicate mathematics content and pedagogy to teachers

- Engage the range of learners in understanding mathematics

Underlying these goals are three guiding principles that are touchstones for the *Investigations* team as we approach both students and teachers as agents of their own learning:

1. *Students have mathematical ideas.* Students come to school with ideas about numbers, shapes, measurements, patterns, and data. If given the opportunity to learn in an environment that stresses making sense of mathematics, students build on the ideas they already have and learn about new mathematics they have never encountered. Students learn that they are capable of having mathematical ideas, applying what they know to new situations, and thinking and reasoning about unfamiliar problems.

2. *Teachers are engaged in ongoing learning* about mathematics content, pedagogy, and student learning. The curriculum provides material for professional development, to be used by teachers individually or in groups, that supports teachers' continued learning as they use the curriculum over several years. The *Investigations* curriculum materials are designed as much to be a dialogue with teachers as to be a core of content for students.

3. *Teachers collaborate with the students and curriculum materials* to create the curriculum as enacted in the classroom. The only way for a good curriculum to be used well is for teachers to be active participants in implementing it. Teachers use the curriculum to maintain a clear, focused, and coherent agenda for mathematics teaching. At the same time, they observe and listen carefully to students, try to understand how they are thinking, and make teaching decisions based on these observations.

Investigations is based on experience from research and practice, including field testing that involved documentation of thousands of hours in classrooms, observations of students, input from teachers, and analysis of student work. As a result, the curriculum addresses the learning needs of real students in a wide range of classrooms and communities. The investigations are carefully designed to invite all students into mathematics—girls and boys; members of diverse cultural, ethnic, and language groups; and students with a wide variety of strengths, needs, and interests.

Based on this extensive classroom testing, the curriculum takes seriously the time students need to develop a strong conceptual foundation and skills based on that foundation. Each curriculum unit focuses on an area of content in depth, providing time for students to develop and practice ideas across a variety of activities and contexts that build on each other. Daily guidelines for time spent on class sessions, Classroom Routines (K–3), and Ten-Minute Math (3–5) reflect the commitment to devoting adequate time to mathematics in each school day.

About This Curriculum Unit

This **Curriculum Unit** is one of nine teaching guides in Grade 2. The fourth unit in Grade 2 is *Pockets, Teeth, and Favorite Things.*

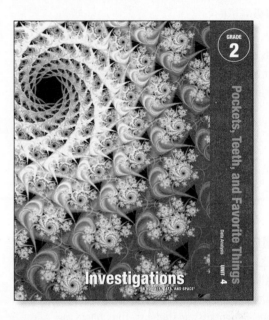

- The **Introduction and Overview** section organizes and presents the instructional materials, provides background information, and highlights important features specific to this unit.

- Each Curriculum Unit contains several **Investigations.** Each Investigation focuses on a set of related mathematical ideas.

- Investigations are divided into one-hour **Sessions,** or lessons.

- Sessions have a combination of these parts: **Activity, Discussion, Math Workshop, Assessment Activity,** and **Session Follow-Up.**

- Each session also has one or more **Classroom Routines** that are done outside of math time.

- At the back of the book is a collection of **Teacher Notes** and **Dialogue Boxes** that provide professional development related to the unit.

- Also included at the back of the book are the **Student Math Handbook** pages for this unit.

- The **Index** provides a way to look up important words or terms.

Overview

OF THIS UNIT

Investigation	Session	Day	
INVESTIGATION 1 **Working with Categorical Data** Students identify and sort data by common attributes. They organize and represent data they collect by playing *Guess My Rule* and taking surveys of their favorite things.	**1.1** Guess My Rule with People	1	
	1.2 Guess My Rule with Yekttis	2	
	1.3 Guess My Rule with Two Rules	3	
	1.4 "Favorite Things"	4	
	1.5 Organizing "Favorite Things" Data	5	
	1.6 Sharing "Favorite Things" Data	6	
	1.7 Assessment: Favorite Foods and Plus 10 Combinations	7	
INVESTIGATION 2 **Pocket and Teeth Data** Students work with numerical data as they collect information about the number of pockets worn by their classmates and the number of teeth lost by second graders and other elementary-age students. Throughout the investigation they organize and represent data.	**2.1** Pocket Towers	8	
	2.2 Pocket Data Representations	9	
	2.3 How Many Teeth Have You Lost?	10	
	2.4 Collecting Teeth Data from Other Classes	11	
	2.5 Representing Teeth Data from Other Classes	12	
	2.6 Comparing Teeth Data	13	
	2.7 Mystery Teeth Data	14	
	2.8 End-of-Unit Assessment	15	

Each *Investigations* session has some combination of these five parts: **Activity, Discussion, Math Workshop, Assessment Activity,** and **Session Follow-Up.** These session parts are indicated in the chart below. Each session also has one **Classroom Routine** that is done outside of math time.

 Ⓦ Interactive Whiteboard

Activity	Discussion	Math Workshop	Assessment Activity	Session Follow-Up
● ●	●			●
Ⓦ Ⓦ Ⓦ				●
Ⓦ ● ●				●
● ●	Ⓦ			●
● ●	Ⓦ			●
●	●			●
Ⓦ			●	●
● Ⓦ	●			●
● ● Ⓦ				●
●	Ⓦ			●
●	Ⓦ			●
● ●				●
●	●			●
Ⓦ ●	●			●
●			Ⓦ	●

Classroom Routines

Quick Images	Today's Number	What Time Is It?
Ⓦ		
	Ⓦ	
		Ⓦ
Ⓦ		
	Ⓦ	
		Ⓦ
Ⓦ		
	Ⓦ	
		Ⓦ
Ⓦ		
	Ⓦ	
		Ⓦ
Ⓦ		
	Ⓦ	
		Ⓦ

Mathematics

IN THIS UNIT

Pockets, Teeth, and Favorite Things is the second-grade unit in the data analysis and probability strand of *Investigations*. In Grades K–5, these units develop ideas about collecting, representing, describing, and interpreting data. In Grades 4–5, they also include ideas about describing and predicting the likelihood of events.

 In Kindergarten and Grade 1, students **LOOKING BACK** engaged in a variety of sorting activities. They carried out many class surveys, often using yes/no questions. An emphasis in Grade 1 was the development of students' own representations of their data. They were also introduced to bar graphs. They described their data, focusing on the number of pieces of data for each category or value, and considered the question "What do the data tell us about your class?"

Students also found the total number of pieces of data in all categories in a data set and discussed its relationship to the total number of students in the class. For example, "If there are 24 students in the class, and everyone was here on the day we took the survey, then we should have 24 pieces of data in all the categories together."

This unit focuses on the following 5 Mathematical Emphases:

1 Data Analysis Sorting and classifying data

Math Focus Points

- Grouping data into categories based on similar attributes
- Sorting the same set of data in different ways
- Sorting a set of data by two attributes at one time

Students' work in this unit begins with a number of sorting activities. They sort the people in their class into different groups according to visible attributes, such as wearing a watch or hair color. They sort a group of mythical creatures, called Yekttis, into groups according to head shape, number

of antennae, and other attributes. Through these activities, students are engaging in a fundamental human activity— classification. They are looking at similarities and differences among individuals in a group and deciding which of many attributes to attend to as they engage in sorting.

Students then apply these ideas to work with categorical data. They work with "messy" sets of data, in which there are many different values. For example, when they ask the question "What is your favorite weekend activity?" they get many different responses (e.g., playing cards, baseball, soccer, reading, playing on the playground, riding a bike, or drawing). Organizing these data by each separate value may result in a long listing of data that does not provide much information (e.g., 2 people like reading, 1 person likes baseball, 1 person likes soccer, 1 person likes playing cards, and 2 people like drawing). By *classifying* these data—seeing which data might be grouped together into categories—students can use the same data to see a variety of information. For example, students might classify the data into "indoor and outdoor activities," or into "things you do by yourself, things you do with one friend, and things you do with a group." By looking at different classifications of the same data, students can answer different questions.

2 Data Analysis Representing data

Math Focus Points

- Representing a set of data sorted into categories
- Comparing representations of a set of data
- Using equations to show how the sum of the responses in each category equals the total responses collected
- Using a Venn diagram to represent a sorted set of data
- Ordering, representing, and describing a set of numerical data
- Comparing ways of organizing data
- Representing data on a line plot

Students use a variety of representations in this unit: Venn diagrams, towers of cubes, line plots, and other representations they create on their own. As they develop their own representations, students pay attention to what the data mean and how to organize the data so that they can describe them. Important issues arise from their work, such as these:

- Why it matters that symbols, such as Xs on a line plot, are the same size

- Whether it matters that data are arranged in numerical order

- How to treat values that have no data

By comparing a variety of representations of the same data, they learn how different representations can make different aspects of the data set harder or easier to describe.

In this unit students are introduced to line plots and other frequency distributions in which each piece of data is represented by one symbol (e.g., an X, a square, or a self-stick note). In using this kind of representation, students have to think through the meaning of how numbers are used in describing the data in two different ways:

1. Some numbers indicate the value of a piece of data (I have 8 pockets).

2. Other numbers indicate how often a particular data value occurs (7 children have 8 pockets).

Students are expected to use a Venn diagram with two overlapping circles and to interpret a line plot of numerical data by the end of the unit. See **Teacher Note:** Students' Representations of Numerical Data on page 124 for more on issues that come up in this unit about representing data.

3 Data Analysis **Describing data**

Math Focus Points

- Describing what the data show about the group surveyed

- Interpreting a data representation including a line plot

- Describing important features of a data set

- Describing a set of numerical data

- Comparing two sets of data

- Developing a hypothesis based on a set of data

When data are classified, ordered, and/or represented, students can describe them. In Grade 2, many students describe data by giving counts of the number of pieces of data that occur at each value (e.g., 10 students like indoor activities, 12 students like outdoor activities). Often, students notice the *mode* of a data set—the category or value that has more data than any other category or value—as well as the lowest and highest values. Second graders can begin to describe the data set as a whole, rather than only the counts at each value. Although focusing on the whole data set will be more of an emphasis in Grade 3, second graders should be encouraged to notice what is going on in a data set overall. You can encourage students to notice overall similarities and differences by comparing groups, as students do when they collect data about the number of lost teeth from their own class and from other classes.

As students are describing numerical data, it is particularly important that they keep in mind the meaning of the data in terms of the situation the data represent. Students can become lost in the symbols and numbers on a line plot. When students describe only the numbers (e.g.,"There are 4 at 8 and 5 at 9"), make sure that you ask them what the meaning of those numbers is. You could say, for example, "What do the 4 Xs at 8 tell us about the teeth that people in our class lost?"

4 Data Analysis Designing and carrying out a data investigation

Math Focus Points

◆ Choosing a survey question

◆ Making a plan for collecting data

◆ Making predictions about data to be collected

◆ Collecting and recording data from a survey

◆ Interpreting and sharing results from a data investigation

Data are collected in a context and for a purpose—to learn something you did not know about your world. By making predictions and then collecting their own data, students see how data are used—to answer a question or to give evidence about an issue. Through experiencing an entire data investigation from start to finish, they encounter at their own level many of the same issues encountered by statisticians as they decide how to collect, keep track of, organize, represent, describe, and interpret their data.

In Investigation 1, students develop questions about "Favorite Things"—favorite books, animals, things to eat, and so on—and then collect their own data on the questions they choose. In Investigation 2, students go beyond their own classroom to collect data from different grades about the number of teeth lost. They then represent and compare these data with their own class's data.

5 Computational Fluency Knowing addition combinations to 10 + 10

Math Focus Points

◆ Achieving fluency with the Plus 10 Combinations

To develop efficient computation strategies, students need to become fluent with the addition combinations from $1 + 1$ to $10 + 10$. In this unit, students achieve fluency with the Plus 10 Combinations ($10 + 3$, $10 + 4$, and so on) that were introduced and practiced through a variety of games and activities in the previous units.

This Unit also focuses on

◆ Developing strategies for combining multiple addends

Classroom Routines focus on

◆ Generating equivalent expressions for a number

◆ Developing fluency with addition and subtraction

◆ Using standard notation (+, −, =) to record expressions and write equations

◆ Using clocks as tools for keeping track of and measuring time

◆ Naming, notating, and telling time to the hour, half hour, and quarter hour on digital and analog clocks

◆ Determining what time it will be when given start and elapsed times that are multiples of 15 minutes

◆ Determining the number of minutes in hours, half hours, and quarter hours

◆ Developing and analyzing visual images for quantities

◆ Combining groups of tens and ones

◆ Adding to or subtracting 10 from a 2-digit number

◆ Noticing what happens to the tens place when a multiple of 10 is added to or subtracted from a 2-digit number

◆ Identifying coins and their values

◆ Adding coin amounts

◆ Using standard notation (¢, +, −, =) to write equations

LOOKING FORWARD

In Grade 3, students continue to work with both categorical and numerical data. Their work is focused on seeing a data set as a whole. They describe where data are concentrated and relate those concentrations of data to the whole data set by using phrases such as *more than half* and *less than half.* Through comparing groups, students choose which aspects of the data are most important in describing the data sets, and they use differences or similarities to make arguments based on their data. For the first time, they encounter the median as a measure of center in numerical data. They spend more time designing their own data investigations. They also consider how the questions they pose and the way they conduct their studies affect the resulting data. In Grades 4 and 5, they will continue building their expertise in designing data investigations, describing data, and using these descriptions to compare groups. Students will further develop their understanding of summarizing what is typical or usual in a data set and will learn to use the median as one tool for summarizing data. They will also study probability.

Assessment

IN THIS UNIT

ONGOING ASSESSMENT: Observing Students at Work

The following sessions provide **Ongoing Assessment: Observing Students at Work** opportunities:

- **Session 1.1, pp. 27 and 29**
- **Session 1.2, p. 37**
- **Session 1.3, p. 44**
- **Session 1.4, p. 53**
- **Session 1.5, pp. 57 and 58**

- **Session 1.6, p. 60**
- **Session 1.7, pp. 64 and 65**
- **Session 2.1, p. 75**
- **Session 2.2, pp. 81 and 82**
- **Session 2.3, p. 88**

- **Session 2.5, pp. 94 and 96**
- **Session 2.6, p. 98**
- **Session 2.7, pp. 104 and 106**
- **Session 2.8, p. 110**

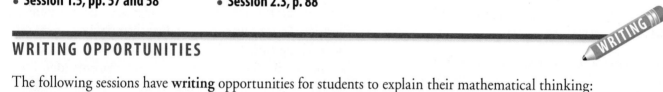

WRITING OPPORTUNITIES

The following sessions have **writing** opportunities for students to explain their mathematical thinking:

- **Session 1.6, p. 60**
  Student Activity Book, p. 8

- **Session 2.3, p. 87**
  Student Activity Book, p. 20

- **Session 2.5, p. 95**
  Student Activity Book, p. 24

- **Session 2.6, p. 98**
  Student Activity Book, p. 27

- **Session 2.7, p. 105**
  Student Activity Book, p. 32

PORTFOLIO OPPORTUNITIES

The following sessions have work appropriate for a **portfolio:**

- **Session 1.5, pp. 57 and 58**
  Favorite Things Representation

- **Session 1.6, p. 60**
  Student Activity Book, p. 8

- **Session 1.7, p. 64**
  Favorite Food Representation and
  M47–M48, Assessment: What Is Your
  Favorite Food?

- **Session 2.2, p. 81**
  Student Activity Book, p. 18

- **Session 2.5, pp. 93 and 95**
  Teeth Data Representations and
  Student Activity Book, pp. 24–25

- **Session 2.7, p. 102**
  Today's Number: 44

- **Session 2.7, p. 105**
  Student Activity Book, p. 32

- **Session 2.8, p. 109**
  M57–M59, End-of-Unit Assessment

Assessing the Benchmarks

Observing students as they engage in conversation about their ideas is a primary means to assess their mathematical understanding. Consider all of your students' work, not just the written assessments. See the chart below for suggestions about key activities to observe.

See the **Differentiation and Intervention Guide** for quizzes that can be used after each Investigation.

Benchmarks in This Unit	Key Activities to Observe	Assessment
1. Use a Venn diagram to sort data by two attributes.	**Session 1.3:** *Guess My Rule* with Two Rules **Session 1.7:** *Guess My Rule* with Animals	**Session 2.8 End-of-Unit Assessment:** Problem 3
2. Identify categories for a set of categorical data and organize the data into chosen categories.	**Session 1.2:** *Guess My Rule* with Yekttis **Session 1.4:** *Guess My Rule* with People: Multiple Categories **Session 1.5:** Organizing Data Into Categories	**Session 1.7 Assessment Activity:** What's Your Favorite Food?
3. Order and represent a set of numerical data. 4. Describe a numerical data set, including the highest and lowest values and the mode. 5. Read and interpret a variety of representations of numerical and categorical data.	**Session 1.6:** Analyzing "Favorite Things" Data **Session 2.1:** Organizing Pocket Towers **Session 2.2:** How Many Pockets Altogether? **Session 2.5:** Representing Teeth Data from Other Classes **Session 2.7:** Mystery Teeth Data (Benchmark 4 only)	**Session 1.7 Assessment Activity:** What's Your Favorite Food? (Benchmark 5) **Session 2.8 End-of-Unit Assessment:** Problem 1 (Benchmark 3 only) Problem 2 (Benchmark 4 and 5)
6. Compare two sets of numerical data.	**Session 2.6:** Comparing Teeth Data	**Session 2.8 End-of-Unit Assessment:** Problem 2
7. Demonstrate fluency with Plus 10 combinations.		**Session 1.7 Assessment Activity:** Plus Ten Combinations 

✓ Checklist Available

Relating the Mathematical Emphases to the Benchmarks

Mathematical Emphases	Benchmarks
Data Analysis Sorting and Classifying Data	1 and 2
Data Analysis Representing Data	1 and 3
Data Analysis Describing Data	4, 5, 6
Data Analysis Designing and Carrying Out a Data Investigation	2, 3, 4, 5, 6
Computational Fluency Knowing Addition Combinations to 10 + 10	7

Classroom Routines

Classroom Routines offer practice and review of key concepts for this grade level. These daily activities, to be done in ten minutes outside of math class, occur in a regular rotation every 4–5 days. Specific directions for the day's routine are provided in each session. For the full description and variations of each classroom routine see *Implementing Investigations in Grade 2.*

Today's Number

Students use strips and singles, or dimes and pennies, to make Today's Number, and discuss place value as they look for patterns in the combinations of tens and ones. They also solve problems about Today's Number in which different parts are missing. (For example, $8 + \_\_\_\_ = 12$ and $20 - \_\_\_\_ = 12$.)

Math Focus Points

◆ Generating equivalent expressions for a number

◆ Developing fluency with addition and subtraction

◆ Using standard notation $(+, -, =)$ to record expressions and write equations

What Time Is It?

Students determine the number of minutes in a half hour and discuss why 30 minutes is one half of an hour. They also continue to practice telling and notating time to the hour and half hour, and are introduced to telling and notating time to the quarter hour.

Math Focus Points

◆ Using clocks as tools for keeping track of and measuring time

◆ Naming, notating, and telling time to the hour, half hour, and quarter hour on digital and analog clocks

◆ Determining what time it will be when given start and elapsed times that are multiples of 15 minutes

◆ Determining the number of minutes in hours, half hours, and quarter hours

Quick Images

Students view three images, each made from strips and singles, and each 10 or 11 more than the previous one. They compare those images, and the location of the totals (e.g. 14, 24, and 34 or 25, 36, 47) on the number line and 100 chart. Other variations present several Ten Frames or a set of coins, and focus on writing equations that represent the image.

Math Focus Points

◆ Developing and analyzing visual images for quantities

◆ Combining groups of tens and ones

◆ Adding to or subtracting 10 from a 2-digit number

◆ Noticing what happens to the tens place when a multiple of 10 is added to or subtracted from a 2-digit number

◆ Identifying coins and their values

◆ Adding coin amounts

◆ Using standard notation $(¢, +, -, =)$ to write equations

Practice and Review

IN THIS UNIT

Practice and review play a critical role in the *Investigations* program. The following components and features are available to provide regular reinforcement of key mathematical concepts and procedures.

Books	Features	In This Unit . . .
Curriculum Unit	**Classroom Routines** offer practice and review of key concepts for this grade level. These daily activities, to be done in ten minutes outside of math class, occur in a regular rotation every 4–5 days. Specific directions for the day's routine are provided in each session. For the full description and variations of each classroom routine see *Implementing Investigations in Grade 2*.	• **All sessions**
Student Activity Book	**Daily Practice** pages in the *Student Activity Book* provide one of three types of written practice: **reinforcement** of the content of the unit, **ongoing review,** or **enrichment** opportunities. Some Daily Practice pages will also have Ongoing Review items with multiple-choice problems similar to those on standardized tests.	• **All sessions**
	Homework pages in the *Student Activity Book* are an extension of the work done in class. At times they help students prepare for upcoming activities.	• **Session 1.1** • **Session 2.2** • **Session 1.4** • **Session 2.3** • **Session 1.7** • **Session 2.6**
Student Math Handbook	**Math Words and Ideas** in the *Student Math Handbook* are pages that summarize key words and ideas. Most Words and Ideas pages have at least one exercise.	• **Student Math Handbook, pp. 51, 104–111**
	Games pages are found in a section of the *Student Math Handbook*.	• **No games are introduced in this unit.**

Supporting the Range of Learners

The **Differentiation and Intervention Guide** provides Intervention, Extension, and Practice activities for use within each Investigation.

Sessions	1.1	1.2	1.3	1.5	1.6	2.2	2.3	2.5	2.6	2.7	2.8
Intervention	•	•	•	•		•		•	•	•	
Extension	•				•	•					
ELL	•	•	•				•				•

Intervention

Suggestions are made to support and engage students who are having difficulty with a particular idea, activity, or problem.

Extension

Suggestions are made to support and engage students who finish early or may be ready for additional challenge.

English Language Learners (ELL)

In this unit, English Language Learners will need to understand everyday words such as *guess, pocket, rule, tooth/teeth, favorite, indoor,* and *outdoor,* as well as data-related terms such as *attribute, category, graph, information, organize,* and *represent.* You can support English Language Learners by previewing activities, reviewing key concepts and vocabulary, and providing visual demonstrations to clarify their understanding. The Math Words and Ideas pages in the *Student Math Handbook* can be a particularly useful reference for English Language Learners.

At various points, students are asked to classify sets of data according to self-defined categories. You may want to preview this task ahead of time by working with a small group of students to sort a set of objects, such as buttons. This set should include different attributes, such as color, shape, and size. Some of the objects may be identical, while others may be unique. Begin by helping students organize the objects into separate values on a chart or grid. After completing this initial sorting, examine the data together. Help students classify the data according to various categories to illustrate the idea that there may be many different ways to organize the set of data.

Working with the Range of Learners is a set of episodes written by teachers that focuses on meeting the needs of the range of learners in the classroom. In the first section, *Setting up the Mathematical Community,* teachers write about how they create a supportive and productive learning environment in their classrooms. In the next section, *Accommodations for Learning,* teachers focus on specific modifications they make to meet the needs of some of their learners. In the last section, *Language and Representation,* teachers share how they help students use representations and develop language to investigate and express mathematical ideas. The questions at the end of each case provide a starting point for your own reflection or for discussion with colleagues. See *Implementing Investigations in Grade 2* for this set of episodes.

Mathematical Emphases

Data Analysis Sorting and classifying data

Math Focus Points

◆ Grouping data into categories based on similar attributes

◆ Sorting the same set of data in different ways

◆ Sorting a set of data by two attributes at one time

Data Analysis Representing data

Math Focus Points

◆ Representing a set of data sorted into categories

◆ Comparing representations of a set of data

◆ Using equations to show how the sum of the responses in each category equals the total responses collected

◆ Using a Venn diagram to represent a sorted set of data

Data Analysis Describing data

Math Focus Points

◆ Describing what the data show about the group surveyed

Data Analysis Designing and carrying out a data investigation

Math Focus Points

◆ Choosing a survey question

◆ Interpreting and sharing results from a data investigation

This Investigation also focuses on

◆ Achieving fluency with the Plus 10 combinations

Working with Categorical Data

	Student Activity Book	Student Math Handbook	Professional Development: Read Ahead of Time	
SESSION 1.1 p. 24				
Guess My Rule with People Students play *Guess My Rule* with People, sorting people into groups according to a secret rule. They represent the data, compare their representations, and write an equation to go with their data set.	1–2	104	• Mathematics in This Unit, p. 10 • **Teacher Notes:** Assessment: Assessing the Plus Ten Combinations, p. 111; When Students Represent Data, p. 112	
SESSION 1.2 p. 32				
Guess My Rule with Yekttis Students sort and classify Yekttis, a group of fictional creatures related by common sets of attributes, as they play *Guess My Rule* with Yekttis. Students respond to a survey question about their favorite weekend activity and discuss ways to organize the data.	3	51, 105, 106–107, 109	• **Teacher Notes:** Attribute Materials: About the Yektti Cards, p. 113; Sorting, Classifying, and Categorical Data, p. 114	
SESSION 1.3 p. 41				
Guess My Rule with Two Rules Students play *Yektti Guess My Rule* with Two Rules as an introduction to Venn diagrams. Students choose "Favorite Things" survey questions to ask their classmates.	4	105, 106–107, 108	• **Dialogue Box:** This Yektti Fits in Both Groups, p. 135	
SESSION 1.4 p. 48				
"Favorite Things" Students sort the data about their favorite weekend activities in different ways and discuss what they can learn from the data, on the basis of how they are sorted. After responding to a "Favorite Things" questionnaire, students organize data from a round of *Guess My Rule* with People into multiple categories.	5–6	105, 106–107, 109	• **Dialogue Box:** What's Your Favorite Weekend Activity?, p. 137	

Classroom Routines See page 16 for an overview.

See page 16 for an overview.

Quick Images

- T38–T39, *Stickers: Strips and Singles* 🖨
  Cut out images
- T28, *Ten-Frame* Cards (1–10) 🖨
  Cut out ten-frames
- T29, *Ten-Frame* Cards (Tens) 🖨
  Cut out ten-frames

Today's Number

- M44, *Today's Number: 12 with Missing Parts*
  Make copies. (1 per student)
- T41, *Today's Number: 12 with Missing Parts* 🖨

What Time Is It?

- M43, The Clock   Make copies. (1 per student)
- T36, The Clock 🖨
- Student clocks, 1 per pair
- Demonstration clock

Materials to Gather	Materials to Prepare
• **Chart paper** (1 sheet) • **12″ x 18″ paper** (1 per pair/individual) • **Markers, self-stick notes, stick-on dots, cubes, tiles, and other materials for making representations** • **Student set of Plus Ten Addition Cards** (from Unit 3)	• M1–M2, **Family Letter** Make copies. (1 per student)
• **Chart paper** (as needed) • **Self-stick notes or index cards** (1 per student)	• M6–M37, **Large Yektti Cards** Make copies. (1 set) • M38–M41, **Small Yektti Cards** Make copies on card stock or heavy paper, if available. Cut out cards and assemble into sets. (1 set per group) • M42, **Yektti Word Cards** Make copies. Cut out cards and assemble into sets. (1 set per group) • **Yarn loops** Use about 5 feet of yarn to make each loop. (1 per group) • **Chart paper** Title the paper "What is your favorite weekend activity?" • **Chart paper** Title the paper "How can we organize the Favorite Weekend Activity data?"
• **Yarn loops** (1 per group; from Session 1.2) • **Small Yektti Cards** (1 set per group; from Session 1.2) • **Yektti Word Cards** (1 set per group; from Session 1.2) • **Blank paper** (1 sheet per pair)	• **Yarn loops** Make more yarn loops and add to the ones from the previous session. (2 per group) • **Chart paper** Draw two 20-inch diameter non-overlapping circles. • **Chart paper** Draw two 20-inch diameter overlapping circles with an overlap of about 10 inches. (1 sheet per group)
• **Self-stick notes** (as needed) • **Chart paper** (1 sheet) • **Chart: "What's your favorite weekend activity?"** (from Session 1.2) • **Chart: "How can we organize the Favorite Weekend Activity data?"** (from Session 1.2) • **"Favorite Things" survey questions** (from Session 1.3) • **12″ x 18″ paper** (1 sheet per pair; as needed) • **Stick-on dots, self-stick notes, cubes, and other materials for making representations** (1 set per pair; as needed)	• M45, **Circle for** *Guess My Rule* Make copies. (1 or 2 per student) • M46, **Venn Diagram for** *Guess My Rule* Make copies. (1 or 2 per student) • **Class Questionnaire** Title a sheet of paper "'Favorite Things' Questionnaire." List all the "Favorite Things" survey questions from Session 1.3, even if some are the same. Include the names of the students who wrote each question. Leave enough space after each question for students to write a response and their name. If the questions extend beyond one page, continue on a separate page. Make copies. (1 per student) See p. 51.

🖨 Overhead Transparency

Working with Categorical Data, *continued*

	Student Activity Book	Student Math Handbook	Professional Development: Read Ahead of Time	
SESSION 1.5 p. 54				
Organizing "Favorite Things" Data Students sort the Favorite Weekend Activity data one more way and summarize what they found out about students' favorite weekend activities. They organize and represent the data from their "Favorite Things" surveys.	7	106–107, 109		
SESSION 1.6 p. 59				
Sharing "Favorite Things" Data Students analyze their "Favorite Things" data. They write about what they learned from their survey and write an equation that shows the quantities in their categories. They then share with the class what they found out from their survey and how they categorized their data.	8–9	106–107, 109, 111		
SESSION 1.7 p. 62				
Assessment: Favorite Foods and Plus 10 Combinations Students sort animals by attributes as they play *Guess My Rule.* Students complete an assessment in which they categorize and represent a data set about their favorite foods.	10–13	51, 105, 106–107, 108, 109	• **Teacher Note:** Assessment: What's Your Favorite Food?, p. 117	

Materials to Gather	Materials to Prepare
• **Self-stick notes** (as needed) • **Chart: "What's your favorite weekend activity?"** (from Session 1.2) • **Chart: "What We Learned"** (from Session 1.4) • **Index cards, or small pieces of paper** (5 to 10 per pair) • **Envelopes** (1 per pair) • **Paper clips** (as needed) • **12″ x 18″ paper** (1 per pair) • **Stick-on dots, self-stick notes, cubes, and other materials for making representations** (as needed)	• **"Favorite Things" questionnaires** Cut the questionnaires from Session 1.4 into strips. Each strip includes the pair's names, their question, and the student's name and response. Sort the strips by the pair that asked the question.
• **Small Yektti Cards** (from Session 1.2; optional) • **Yektti Word Cards** (from Session 1.2; optional) • **Chart paper with a Venn diagram on it or two yarn loops** (from Session 1.3; optional) • **"Favorite Things" data representations** (1 per pair; from Session 1.5)	
• **Chart paper** (2 sheets; optional) • **Blank paper** (1 sheet per student) • **Scissors** (optional)	• **M45, Circle for *Guess My Rule*** Make copies. (as needed) • **M46, Venn Diagram for *Guess My Rule*** Make copies. (as needed) • **M47–M48, Assessment: What's Your Favorite Food?** Make copies. (1 per student) • **M49–M50, Family Letter** Make copies. (1 per student) • **M51, Assessment Checklist: Plus 10 Combinations** Make copies. (as needed) ✓

✓ Checklist Available

Guess My Rule with People

Math Focus Points

◆ Grouping data into categories based on similar attributes

◆ Representing a set of data sorted into categories

◆ Comparing representations of a set of data

◆ Using equations to show how the sum of the responses in each category equals the total responses collected

Vocabulary
data
rule
representation

Today's Plan		Materials
① ACTIVITY *Guess My Rule* with People 20 MIN CLASS		• Chart paper
② ACTIVITY Representing the Data 25 MIN PAIRS INDIVIDUALS		• 12″ x 18″ paper; markers, self-stick notes, stick-on dots, cubes, tiles, and other materials for making representations; student set of Plus 10 Addition Cards from Unit 3
③ DISCUSSION Representations and Equations 15 MIN CLASS		• *Guess My Rule* representations (from previous activity)
④ SESSION FOLLOW-UP Daily Practice and Homework		• *Student Activity Book,* pp. 1–2 • *Student Math Handbook,* p. 104 • M1–M2, Family Letter*

*See *Materials to Prepare,* p. 21.

Classroom Routines

Quick Images: Strips and Singles Using *Stickers: Strips and Singles* (T38–T39), display the number 14 with 1 strip and 4 singles. Follow the basic *Quick Images* activity. Have pairs discuss how many squares they saw and how they determined the amount. Repeat with the numbers 24 and 34. As a class, find 14, 24, and 34 on the number line and 100 chart and discuss what is the same and different about them. If time permits, repeat with the numbers 22, 32, and 42.

ACTIVITY

1 *Guess My Rule* with People

20 MIN   CLASS

For the next few weeks, we'll be collecting information or **data** about one another. We will be thinking about how to put our data into categories—something that scientists and mathematicians often do—and we will be looking at different ways to collect, organize, and show our data.

Today, we are going to play *Guess My Rule* with People.❶ We are going to group the people in our class into categories by attributes that they have in common. I am going to think of a **rule** that fits some of you, but not all of you. I am going to write down my rule so that I don't forget it, and I am going to keep it secret for now.❷

Choose a straightforward, visually obvious rule that fits some of the students, but not all of them. For example, you may choose "wearing striped shirts." Write your rule in large letters on a piece of paper, but do not show it to the class.

I am going to ask the people who fit my rule to stand over here. (Point to one section of the classroom.) And I'm going to ask the people who don't fit my rule to stand over there. (Point to another section of the room.)

Ask two students who fit your rule to stand in one area, and ask one student who does not fit your rule to stand in the other.

These two people fit my rule. (Point to the two students you've selected who fit your rule.) This person does not fit my rule. (Point to the one student you selected who does not fit your rule.) Don't try to guess my rule yet! Instead, can you tell me someone else who you think might or might not fit my rule?

Students take turns suggesting class members who they think may or may not fit your rule. Each time, announce whether the selected student fits your rule and send that student to the appropriate group.

Teaching Note

❶ ***Guess My Rule . . . Again*** Many students in the class may have played *Guess My Rule* in Grade 1. You may want to begin by asking them to recall the rules of the game.

Differentiation

❷ **English Language Learners** To prepare English Language Learners to play *Guess My Rule* with the class, play a few rounds with them ahead of time, emphasizing key vocabulary such as *rule*, *guess*, and *fit*. (If you have only a small number of English Language Learners in your classroom, include a few of their native English-speaking classmates in this group.) Today we're going to play a game about *rules*. Rules tell us what we should and should not do. I'm going to think of a rule about who should sit at the left side of the table, and you're going to try to *guess* what the rule is. **Place two boys at the left side of the table and one girl at the right.** Alberto and Chen *fit* my rule, but Yama *does not fit* my rule. Who else would *fit* my rule? Who else should sit over here with Alberto and Chen? **Continue thinking aloud until a few more children have been assigned to the appropriate groups.** What rule did I use to decide who should sit over here? Can anybody *guess* my rule? **Repeat the activity, using more subtle characteristics.** Then invite students to think of their own rules for others to guess. If time does not allow you to meet with English Language Learners beforehand, you can still emphasize the key vocabulary and keep the above suggestion in mind as you play *Guess My Rule* with the whole class.

❸ **Rules You Can See** Students should understand that you are grouping people by a characteristic that everyone can see, such as hair color or clothing—not by a characteristic that cannot be seen, such as "likes chocolate" or "has a dog."

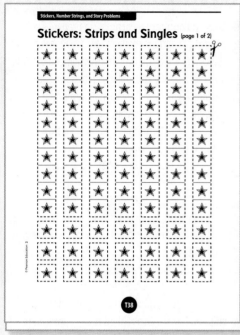

Stickers, Number Strings, and Story Problems

Stickers: Strips and Singles (page 1 of 2)

T38

▲ Transparencies, T38–T39

The class sorts students into groups according to a rule.

If no one suggests a person who they think does *not* fit the rule after a few people have been sorted, ask:

Do you think there is anyone who does *not* fit my rule? Finding out who does not fit the rule is just as important as finding out who does. It gives you important information that will help you figure out my rule.❸

Students continue with their suggestions until most of them have been sorted. At this point, ask for volunteers to share what they think your rule is and why. Once students have guessed your rule, show students your piece of paper with the rule on it.

Ask the students who are still in their seats to move to the group where they belong. Count the number of students in each group. Display a sheet of chart paper and record the data about the number of people in each group (e.g., wearing striped shirts: 8, not wearing striped shirts: 17). Ask students to return to their seats.

As we played this game, we collected some data on students in this class. We found out that [8 students are wearing striped shirts today] and that [17 students are not wearing striped shirts]. Let's see what else we can find out about students in this class.

Continue playing three or four more rounds of *Guess My Rule* with People, giving students the opportunity to choose the mystery rule and lead the game. For example, rules might include "wearing a watch/not wearing a watch" or "wearing shoelaces/not wearing shoelaces." At the end of each round, record the results on the sheet of chart paper. This information will be used in the next activity.

Wearing a striped shirt	8
Not wearing a striped shirt	17
Wearing a watch	10
Not wearing a watch	15
Wearing shoelaces	16
Not wearing shoelaces	9
Wearing glasses	4
Not wearing glasses	21

ONGOING ASSESSMENT: Observing Students at Work

- **Are students able to sort people according to common attributes?**

- **Do students identify people who do not fit the rule?**

ACTIVITY

25 MIN   PAIRS   INDIVIDUALS

2 Representing the Data

We just collected some interesting information, or data, about our class. We found out how many people are [wearing striped shirts today] and how many people are [not wearing striped shirts]. We found out how many people are [wearing a watch] today and how many people are [not wearing a watch].

Mathematicians have different ways of showing the data they collect so that they can see it clearly and share it with other people. Sometimes they make pictures or models, and sometimes they make graphs. These are all representations of data. ④

Have students generate ideas about how they might make a representation of data. Use a set of data from the previous activity as an example, such as "wearing a watch/not wearing a watch." Ask students how they might organize a picture or graph and what materials they might use. Show some of their ideas on chart paper.

Teaching Note

④ **Define** *representation*   The word *representation* may be unfamiliar to students. Use words such as *picture, graph, chart,* or *model* along with it to help students understand its meaning.

Working in pairs or individually, students will choose one of the rules from the previous activity. They will use markers, self-stick notes, stick-on dots, cubes, tiles, or other materials that you provide to represent the data from that rule on a large sheet of paper. Students will

- write the rule

- show how many people fit the rule and how many do not

- write how many people are in each group

Encourage students to make a representation that communicates clearly to others what they found out. You may want to talk briefly about shortcuts for representing data.

It might take a long time to draw 10 hands with watches and 15 hands without watches. What might be some shortcut ways of showing the data so that you don't have to spend too much time drawing?

When the students have finished their representations, display them.

Sample Student Work

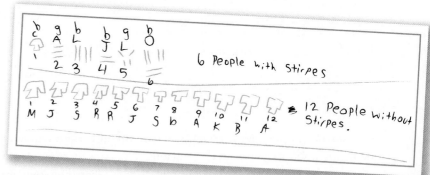

Sample Student Work

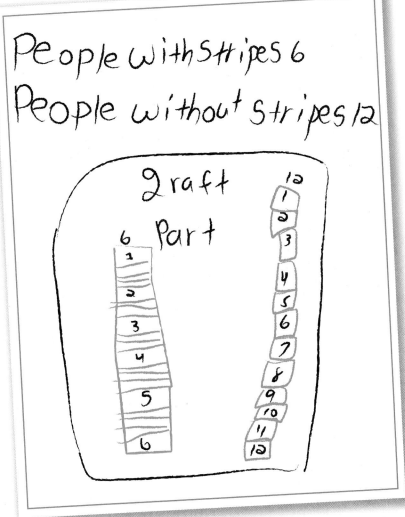

Sample Student Work

ONGOING ASSESSMENT: Observing Students at Work

While students are working, circulate through the class, observe how they make a representation of data, and ask them to explain their representations to you.

- **Are students making clear representations of the sorted groups?** Are they organizing the information so that the two groups are distinct?

- **Can students represent the data visually and numerically?**

- **Can students interpret their representations?** Can they extract the important information from their representations?

Professional Development

⑤ **Teacher Note:** When Students Represent Data, p. 112

DIFFERENTIATION: Supporting the Range of Learners

Extension Students who quickly finish making a clear and accurate representation can make a different kind of representation of the same data set or can make a representation of another data set.

Intervention Some students may get so bogged down in drawing individual people that they are not able to represent the amount of data accurately. Encourage these students to use other materials, such as stick-on dots or notes, to lessen the burden of drawing.⑤

DISCUSSION

③ Representations and Equations

15 MIN · **CLASS**

Math Focus Points for Discussion

◈ Comparing representations of a set of data

◈ Using equations to show how the sum of the responses in each category equals the total responses collected

To begin this discussion, have students look around at all the *Guess My Rule* with People representations and share their observations.

How are the representations you made the same? How are they different?

Students may notice that

• Students represented the data in different ways;

• The quantities in the two groups are different when students represented different rules;

• The quantities in the two groups are the same when students represented the same rule.

Can you think of an equation that you could write that would show how many students fit the rule you chose, how many students do not fit the rule you chose, and how many students there are in total?

Write a volunteer's equation on the board. Ask what each number stands for and label it.

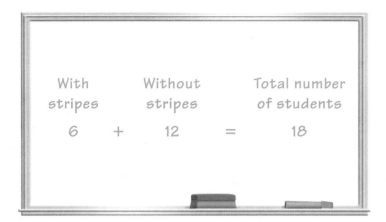

With stripes		Without stripes		Total number of students
6	+	12	=	18

Have pairs or individuals write their representation as an equation that fits their data set. Ask pairs or individuals to share their equations with the class and write them on the board. All of the equations should have the same total. If not, discuss the different totals.

Why do all the equations have the same total? Why do some equations have the same addends and some do not have the same addends?

It should come up that the "total" represents the number of students in class on that day. No matter how the class is sorted, the total number of people will always be the same.

SESSION FOLLOW-UP

4 Daily Practice and Homework

 Daily Practice: For ongoing review, have students complete *Student Activity Book* page 1.

 Homework: On *Student Activity Book* page 2, students are given some of the quantities from a round of *Guess My Rule* with People. They need to figure out the missing quantities.

 Student Math Handbook: Students and families may use *Student Math Handbook* page 104 for reference and review. See pages 145–147 in the back of this unit.

 Family Letter: Send home copies of the Family Letter (M1–M2).

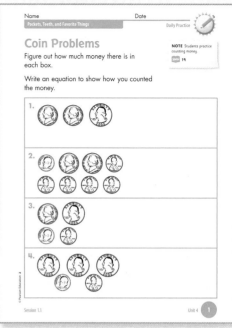

▲ **Student Activity Book, p. 1**

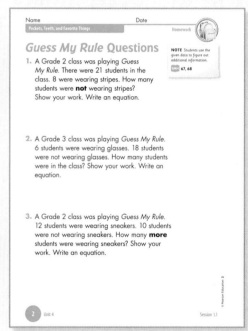

▲ **Student Activity Book, p. 2**

Guess My Rule with Yekttis

Math Focus Points

◆ Grouping data into categories based on similar attributes

◆ Sorting the same set of data in different ways

Vocabulary

attribute
category

Today's Plan		Materials
ACTIVITY **① Introducing Yekttis** — 20 MIN, CLASS		• M6–M37* • Chart paper
ACTIVITY **② Guess My Rule with Yekttis** — 25 MIN, CLASS, GROUPS		• M38–M41*; M42* • Yarn loops (optional)*
ACTIVITY **③ Introducing "What's Your Favorite Weekend Activity?"** — 15 MIN, CLASS		• Self-stick notes or index cards; chart papers titled "What's your favorite weekend activity?" and "How can we organize the Favorite Weekend Activity data?"*; chart paper
SESSION FOLLOW-UP **④ Daily Practice and Homework**		• *Student Activity Book*, p. 3 • *Student Math Handbook*, pp. 51, 105, 106–107, 109

*See *Materials to Prepare,* p. 21.

Classroom Routines

Today's Number: 53 Using Strips and Singles Together as a class, use *Stickers:* Strips and Singles (T38–T39), to represent the number 53. Challenge the class to find all possible combinations. (There are 6 if you include 0 strips and 53 singles.) List the combinations and discuss what students notice, paying particular attention to how the number of singles decreases by 10 when a strip is added.

ACTIVITY

20 MIN   CLASS

1 Introducing Yekttis

Read the following story, "A Strange Discovery," to start off this session:

Amanda and Ari, eight-year-old twins, discovered some strange creatures near their home in Wyoming. These creatures were living in abandoned prairie dog burrows next to a dirt road that the twins used as a shortcut to school. Amanda and Ari started studying these creatures. They visited them every chance they had. Because these creatures never came all the way out of their holes in the ground, Amanda and Ari could only see their heads. The creatures looked as though they might have come from another planet.

Ari loved to make up codes and learn about languages. After a few months, he learned how to say some words in the creatures' own language, and he taught them a few words in English and in Spanish. He learned that the creatures called themselves Yekttis (YEK-tees), that they came from a very distant planet, and that they were peaceful.

Amanda liked to study different kinds of living things. She decided to do a report about the Yekttis for a science project at school. She made a sketch of the head of each of the Yekttis she had seen. She noticed that many of them were similar to one another, but that no two were exactly alike. She used her sketches to figure out how she could describe to other human beings what the Yekttis looked like.

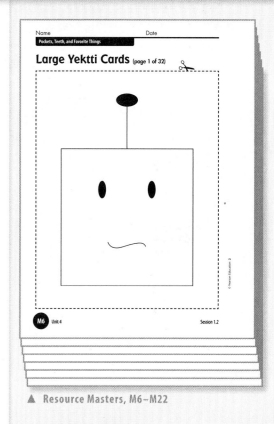

▲ Resource Masters, M6–M22

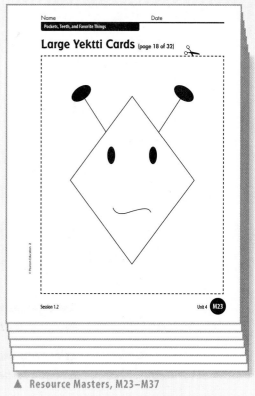

▲ Resource Masters, M23–M37

Professional Development

❶ **Teacher Note:** Attribute Materials: About the Yektti Cards, p. 113

Teaching Notes

❷ **Yektti Attributes** Three attributes vary from Yektti to Yektti: number of antennae, head shape, and eye type.

❸ **One Attribute at a Time** At first, students may have difficulty concentrating on more than one attribute at a time. Consider choosing Yekttis with the same head shape until students start to recognize different eye types and numbers of antennae.

Today we will look at copies of Amanda's sketches and then try to describe the Yekttis.❶

I'm going to show you some Yekttis one at a time. Here's the first one. (Show one of the large Yektti Cards). What can you tell me about what a Yektti looks like? Here's another one. What do you see that's the same as or different from the first one?

Remember that Amanda and Ari found out that the Yekttis are similar, but no two are exactly alike.

As students expand their descriptions, gradually reveal more Yektti Cards. Then ask students to discuss the creatures' attributes.❷

You've seen quite a few of the Yekttis and you've made some observations about them. Can you describe a Yektti that you think I might have a card for? Juanita said this one has a square head and three antennae. Can anyone think of another one I might have that's like it, but is not exactly the same?

To stress the informational nature of each student's contribution, rather than whether a particular description is "correct," respond with another piece of information. For example,

Students might say:

 "Do you have a Yektti with a square head and five antennae?"

You could respond:

No, but I have one with a square head with four antennae.❸

Keep the Yekttis that students have identified along the chalkboard ledge, or have students hold them up in front of the group. Through continued questioning, students gradually determine the attributes of the Yekttis: four head shapes, four numbers of antennae, and two eye types.

After a while, you can ask students to specify all three attributes of the Yektti that they want to see.

Students might say:

"Do you have a triangle Yektti with one antenna and ringed eyes?"

When the discussion has touched on all the possible combinations of Yektti attributes, ask students to summarize these attributes. Make a list of them on a sheet of chart paper.

What different attributes of Yekttis have you noticed? What different types do we have?

There is no need to generate descriptions of all thirty-two of the individual Yekttis, but some classes do enjoy figuring out every one.

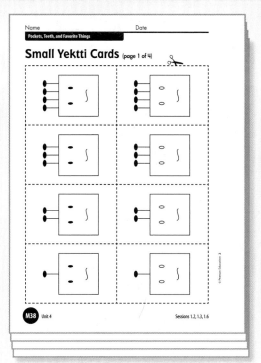

▲ Resource Masters, M38–M41

ACTIVITY

2 *Guess My Rule* with Yekttis

🕐 25 MIN   👥 CLASS   👥 GROUPS

In our last session, we played *Guess My Rule* with People. Today, we will play *Guess My Rule* with Yekttis, using a set of Small Yektti Cards (M38–M41) and a set of Yektti Word Cards (M42).

Go through the word cards with students to make sure that they can identify the different attributes. Explain that later they will break into groups of three or four. Members of each group will take turns choosing a mystery rule, such as "plain eyes" or "antennae," and find its matching word card. Students also may select a random word card.

Lead one round to show how it works. Choose a word card (e.g., "4 antennae") and place it face down. Spread out the small Yektti cards face up. Set out a yarn loop or a piece of paper. Place two Yekttis that fit your rule within the loop or on the paper.

These Yekttis fit my rule. (Point to the cards in the loop or on the paper.)

Put two Yekttis cards that do not fit your rule out of the loop or off the paper, but close by.

These Yekttis don't fit my rule. (Point to the cards you placed outside the loop or off the paper.) If you think you know my rule, don't guess it yet! Instead, show me a Yektti that you think fits or doesn't fit my rule.

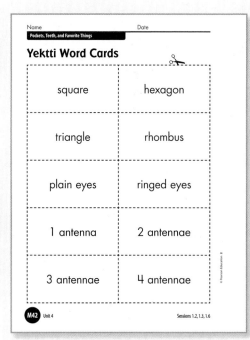

▲ Resource Masters, M42

Teaching Note

❹ **Encourage Educated Guesses** Remind groups that they should be pretty sure about the mystery rule before they make a guess.

After a student places a Yektti card, confirm that this is the correct location for the card or move it.

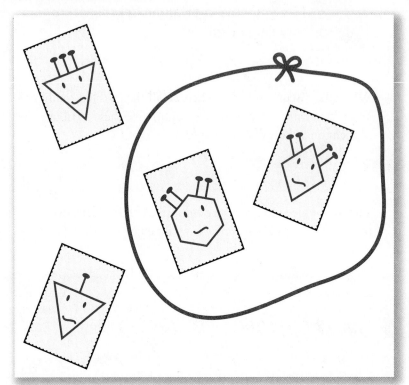

Make sure that you look carefully at the Yekttis that don't fit my rule as well as those that do. They will give you important information.

Continue playing until most students seem to know the rule. Have a student guess the rule and then show your rule card. ❹

Explain to students that they will play *Guess My Rule* with Yekttis in groups of 3 or 4. Every group member should have at least one turn choosing the mystery rule.

As students play, help them think about where they are placing the Yektti cards. Encourage them to use the already-sorted Yekttis as evidence to help them place the remaining cards. Ask the following questions:

• Why do think that Yektti belongs there?

• Which Yektti do you think does not fit the rule?

ONGOING ASSESSMENT: Observing Students at Work

As students play the game, observe how they sort a set of data according to its attributes.

- **Do students correctly sort the objects according to a rule?**

- **Do students make systematic choices of where to place the Yektti cards on the basis of evidence from the already-sorted Yektti cards?**

- **Do they use positive information (those that fit the rule) and negative information (those that do not fit the rule)?**

DIFFERENTIATION: Supporting the Range of Learners

Intervention Some students may find it difficult to focus on a single common attribute. For example, if three Yekttis have the same number of antennae but differently-shaped heads, students may not recognize that they fit together. To help, choose two Yektti cards that have two common attributes and one different attribute. Ask students these questions:

How are these Yekttis the same? How are they different?

Repeat with two Yektti cards that have one common attribute and two that are different.

Intervention Sometimes, the "rule choosers" consistently assign Yekttis to the wrong group. Ask these students to double-check their placement decisions. They should look carefully at their rule and then at the Yekttis in the loop to make sure that the cards in the loop all share the mystery attribute. Then they should look again at the Yekttis outside the loop to make sure that they do not share it.

ELL While this activity provides good visual support for English Language Learners, they may need some language support in order to participate fully in the activity. You can meet with a group of English Language Learners ahead of time to introduce descriptive words such as *square, triangular,* and *hexagonal* and the names of Yektti body parts such as *head, eyes,* and *antennae.* You might also want to make copies of several Yektti cards that English Language Learners can label with the key vocabulary and use for reference during the whole-class activity.

ACTIVITY

Introducing "What's Your Favorite Weekend Activity?"

15 MIN CLASS

This short activity introduces students to the survey work that they will be doing in subsequent sessions. Students will continue to do some *Guess My Rule* activities as they begin working on surveys.

One way that data can be useful is to help us learn more about the people around us. When we played *Guess My Rule* with People, we learned a little about the people in this class. We could learn more by taking a survey. During the next few days you are going to take surveys about your favorite things.

Today, we are going to take a survey about favorite weekend activities. Think for a minute about this question: "What is your favorite weekend activity?" Your favorite activity could be something you do inside your home or outside, with a relative, a friend, or by yourself.

Have students write their responses on self-stick notes or index cards in big letters. Show students the chart paper you have titled "What is your favorite weekend activity?"

Collect the self-stick notes and put them up randomly on the chart paper so that all the students can see.

What do you notice about the data that we collected? What can we say about the class' favorite weekend activities according to these data?

It may be hard for students to notice any similarities before you organize the data, but some may see a few. They may recognize that many people like to do outdoor activities or that students prefer to do things with their parents instead of alone. Write these types of generalizations, along with the categories that students used to group the data.

You were able to notice some things about the data, but we could probably learn more if we organized the data in some way. Can you think of a way that we could organize them that would show us something about the different types of favorite weekend activities?

Write some of the students' suggestions on chart paper. If no one comes up with putting the activities into categories based on similarities, bring it up as a possible way to organize the data.⑤

When mathematicians work with data, they usually put the data into categories to help them learn something about the data. When we played Guess My Rule, *we put things into categories: people with striped shirts, people without striped shirts, people wearing watches, people not wearing watches, Yekttis with three antennae, and so on.*

Think about some ways we could put our new data into categories to help us figure out which types of activities are favorites of students in this class. What are some categories we could use? How are some of these activities similar?

Post the chart paper titled "How can we organize the Favorite Weekend Activity data?" that you prepared ahead of time. If students do not understand what you mean by categories, give an example and then write their suggestions. They may suggest the following:

- Outdoor activities and indoor activities;

- Activities done alone, with friends, with relatives;

- Activities in which you move a lot or a little.

Professional Development

⑤ **Teacher Note:** Sorting, Classifying, and Categorical Data, p. 114

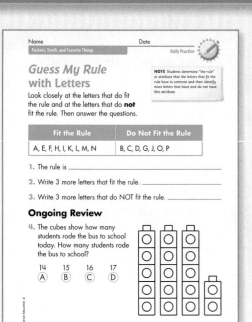

▲ **Student Activity Book, p. 3**

How can we organize the Favorite Weekend Activity data?

In a line

Categories

Outdoor/Indoor

Activities in which you are moving often/moving a little/not moving

Sports/Reading/TV/Games/Eating

In a few days, we will organize our data in some of the ways that you suggested. Then we will see what we can learn about the favorite weekend activities of students in this class.

Save students' responses to "What is your favorite weekend activity?" and "How can we organize the Favorite Weekend Activity data?" to use in Session 1.4.

SESSION FOLLOW-UP

4 Daily Practice and Homework

 Daily Practice: For reinforcement of this unit's content, have students complete *Student Activity Book* page 3.

 Homework: Students should continue to use their Addition Combination cards to practice and review the Plus 10 Combinations (and any other addition combinations they are still working on from previous units). Achieving fluency with these combinations is a Benchmark for this unit.

Student Math Handbook: Students and families may use *Student Math Handbook* pages 51, 105, 106–107, 109 for reference and review. See pages 145–147 in the back of this unit.

Guess My Rule with Two Rules

Math Focus Points

◆ Sorting a set of data by two attributes at one time

◆ Using a Venn diagram to represent a sorted set of data

◆ Choosing a survey question

Venn diagram
survey

Today's Plan		Materials
ACTIVITY **① Introducing Venn Diagrams** 15 MIN · CLASS		• Small Yektti Cards • Chart paper or yarn loops*
ACTIVITY **② Yektti Guess My Rule with Two Rules** 30 MIN · GROUPS		• M38–M41; M42 • Chart paper or yarn*
ACTIVITY **③ Choosing a "Favorite Things" Survey Question** 15 MIN · CLASS · PAIRS		
SESSION FOLLOW-UP **④ Daily Practice**		• *Student Activity Book*, p. 4 • *Student Math Handbook*, pp. 105, 106–107, 108

*See *Materials to Prepare*, p. 21.

Classroom Routines

What Time is It?: Counting the Minutes Using The Clock (M43) students divide a clock in half by drawing a line between the 12 and the 6. Students then count the number of minutes on each half and on the clock as a whole. Show the transparency of The Clock (T36), and discuss why 30 minutes is half an hour.

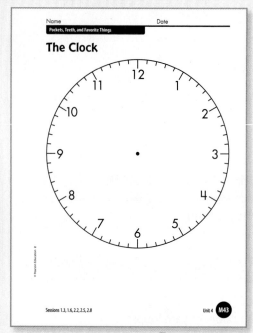

Name _____ Date _____

Pockets, Teeth, and Favorite Things

The Clock

Sessions 1.3, 1.6, 2.2, 2.5, 2.8   Unit 4 **M43**

▲ **Resource Masters, M43; T36**

15 MIN   CLASS

ACTIVITY

① Introducing Venn Diagrams

Ask students to gather around you on the floor or at a table where you have placed a sheet of chart paper with two non-intersecting circles on it. Alternatively, you can use two separate yarn loops.

Play *Guess My Rule* with the class, using a set of Small Yektti Cards and Yektti Word Cards from the previous session. For this game, choose 2 Word Cards.

- Spread out the Small Yektti Cards face up.

- Choose two Word Cards (e.g., "hexagon" and "3 antennae").

- Place one Word Card, face down, in each circle.

- Place one Yektti Card that fits each rule, face up, in each circle, and two Yektti Cards that do not fit the rule outside the circles.

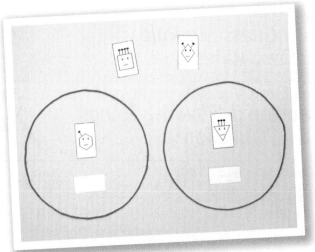

Students play Guess My Rule *with small Yektti Cards.*

Students specify which circles they think a card belongs in. Have them place Yekttis that they think do not fit either rule in a visible space outside the circles. If a student places a card that does not fit in the specified circle, you might say this:

- That Yektti does not fit the circle you chose, but it does fit the other circle.

- That Yektti doesn't fit the circle you chose, or the other circle, so I'll place it outside of the circles.

Students may have a card with the Yekttis that have both attributes. If they are uncertain where to place the card, encourage them to suggest ways to address the situation.❶

How should we show when a card fits both rules?

Some students might suggest creating a third circle or they might suggest placing the cards so that they touch both circles. Follow through with their suggestions.

When students guess the mystery rules, turn over the Word Cards and continue to sort the remaining cards.

When the game is over, display a second a sheet of chart paper, one with overlapping circles (or overlap the yarn loops).

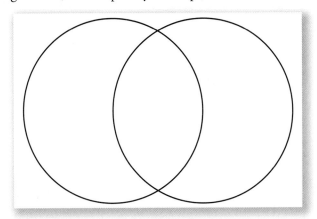

These overlapping circles make a **Venn diagram.**❷ A Venn diagram is a picture that mathematicians use to show things that belong in more than one group. The place in the middle is inside both circles, so it fits both rules. If we look at the Yekttis in the game we just played, which ones belong in the middle?

After students sort all the cards, ask them to describe what they see.

• Which Yekttis can go only in the left circle? How did you figure that out?

• Which can go only in the right circle?

• Which go in the middle?

• Which Yekttis can't go in either of the circles? How do you know?

Professional Development

❶ **Dialogue Box:** This Yektti Fits in Both Groups, p. 135

Differentiation

❷ **English Language Learners** In order to understand and discuss Venn diagrams, English Language Learners must be familiar with words that describe position, such as *left, right, middle, inside,* and *outside.* You can teach these words with a physical demonstration. Place two large, overlapping circles of yarn (or two overlapping hula-hoops) on the floor, and demonstrate various positions in relation to them. I'm standing *outside* the circles. Now I'm standing *inside* the *left* circle. Tia, please stand *inside* the *right* circle. Juan, please stand in the *middle* inside both circles. Now let's all step *outside* the circles. Repeat the demonstration using other students. Then have students take turns telling each other where to stand in relation to the circles.

ACTIVITY

Yektti Guess My Rule with Two Rules

Students form groups of three or four to play *Guess My Rule* with Yekttis, using two mystery rules. Each group will use a sheet of chart paper, with a Venn diagram or two overlapping yarn loops on it. Each person in the group will have a chance to select the mystery rules by choosing two Yektti Word Cards and placing them face down, one in each circle.

As you circulate, remind students that the middle section of the diagram is really inside both circles and is the place for Yekttis that fit both rules. Sometimes no Yekttis will fit in the middle (e.g., when students choose "triangular head" and "hexagonal head" as rules). Point out that these are still legitimate rules.

Many analytical skills are used in this game. You may notice the following:

- Students may be able to place the cards accurately but may not be able to verbalize the descriptions of each group.

- Students may be able to describe the groups after they have been formed, but may not be as good at using evidence to classify the cards during the course of the game.

- Students may have difficulty recognizing which cards fit both rules and may put those cards in one of the one-rule sections.

The more students work with sorting a set by two attributes, the more familiar they will become with these ideas.

ONGOING ASSESSMENT: Observing Students at Work

As students play *Yektti Guess My Rule* with Two Rules, observe how they sort sets of data by using two attributes.

- **Do students sort the Yektti cards according to the chosen rules?**

- **Are students able to identify when a Yektti fits both rules and place it appropriately?**

- **Do students use the Yekttis that are already sorted as evidence to help them choose the next card?**

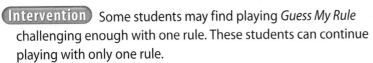

DIFFERENTIATION: Supporting the Range of Learners

Intervention Some students may find playing *Guess My Rule* challenging enough with one rule. These students can continue playing with only one rule.

Intervention Some students may benefit from looking more closely at each circle in the Venn diagram. For example, if the rules are "square" and "2 antennae," you might cover up the "square" part of the circle and direct the students to look at the whole circle for "2 antennae."

- What is the same about all of the cards in the circle? (They all have 2 antennae.)

- What is different about the ones in the middle? (They have 2 antennae and they are square.)

Next, cover up the area for "2 antennae" and look at the whole circle for "square." Ask the same questions. This may help students see the purpose of the overlap and the relationships between the different parts.

Students place cards that fit both rules in the overlap of the two circles.

ACTIVITY

③ Choosing a "Favorite Things" Survey Question

In the next few sessions, students will be taking surveys about their favorite things. In this session, students will decide what their survey questions will be.

In our last math class, we collected data from a survey about your favorite weekend activities. Can someone tell us what a survey is?

Over the next few days, we're going to collect data about our favorite things. These surveys will give us an opportunity to learn more about those things and about one another. Let's think together about some interesting questions you could ask your classmates to learn about their favorite things.

Brainstorm possible questions for the "Favorite Things" survey. Encourage students to share questions that will yield interesting data. Questions such as "What is your favorite number?" or "What is your favorite color?" are fun to ask, but you cannot learn much from the responses about the people you are surveying. If students are unsure of good questions to ask, here are some suggestions:

What is your favorite book?

What is your favorite food to eat for dinner?

What is your favorite place in your home?

What is your favorite thing to wear?

What is your favorite place to go in the summer?

What is your favorite animal?

What is your favorite activity to do during recess?

What is your favorite thing to do at school?

Explain to students that they will work with a partner to choose a "Favorite Things" survey question to ask their classmates. They can choose one of the questions from the class list or come up with a different question. Each pair should write its question and students' names on a piece of paper and hand it to you. Check in with each pair to make sure that the questions will yield interesting responses.

When students have finished, collect and save their questions. You will be using them to create a questionnaire in Session 1.4. See page 51 for an example.

SESSION FOLLOW-UP
4 Daily Practice

 Daily Practice: For ongoing review, have students complete *Student Activity Book* page 4.

 Student Math Handbook: Students and families may use *Student Math Handbook* pages 105, 106–107, 108 for reference and review. See pages 145–147 in the back of this unit.

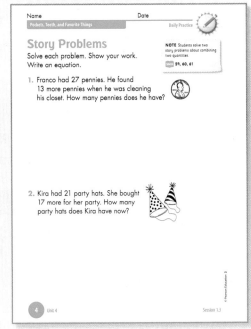

Name _____ Date _____

Pockets, Teeth, and Favorite Things   Daily Practice

Story Problems
Solve each problem. Show your work.
Write an equation.

NOTE Students solve two story problems about combining two quantities

SMH 59, 60, 61

1. Franco had 27 pennies. He found 13 more pennies when he was cleaning his closet. How many pennies does he have?

2. Kira had 21 party hats. She bought 17 more for her party. How many party hats does Kira have now?

4 Unit 4   Session 1.3

▲ **Student Activity Book, p. 4**

"Favorite Things"

Math Focus Points

◆ Sorting the same set of data in different ways

◆ Describing what the data show about the group surveyed

◆ Representing a set of data sorted into categories

Vocabulary

questionnaire

Today's Plan		Materials
① DISCUSSION **What's Your Favorite Weekend Activity?**	🕐 15 MIN 👪 CLASS	• Self-stick notes; chart papers "What's your Favorite Weekend Activity?" and "How can we organize the Favorite Weekend Activity data?" (from Session 1.2); chart paper
② ACTIVITY **Filling Out the "Favorite Things" Questionnaire**	🕐 20 MIN 👤 INDIVIDUALS	• "Favorite Things" questionnaire* (from Session 1.3)
③ ACTIVITY ***Guess My Rule* with People: Multiple Categories**	🕐 25 MIN 👪 CLASS 👫 PAIRS	• 12″ x 18″ paper; stick-on dots, self-stick notes, cubes, and other materials for making representations
④ SESSION FOLLOW-UP **Daily Practice and Homework**		• *Student Activity Book*, pp. 5–6 • *Student Math Handbook*, pp. 105, 106–107, 109 • M45*, M46*

*See *Materials to Prepare*, p. 21.

Classroom Routines

Quick Images: Strips and Singles Using *Stickers:* Strips and Singles (T38–T39), display 25 with 2 strips and 5 singles. Follow the basic *Quick Images* activity. Have pairs discuss how they determined the amount of squares. Repeat with the numbers 36 and 47. As a class, find 25, 36, and 47 on the number line and 100 chart and discuss how they are related.

① What's Your Favorite Weekend Activity?

15 MIN   CLASS

Math Focus Points for Discussion

◈ Sorting the same set of data in different ways

◈ Describing what the data show about the group surveyed

Post the charts, "What is your favorite weekend activity?" and "How can we organize the Favorite Weekend Activity data?" from Session 1.2. Choose one of the ways that students suggested organizing the data that has at least two categories.

A few days ago, you took a survey on your favorite weekend activities and these were your responses. (Point to the self-stick notes on the chart paper titled "What is your favorite weekend activity?") We talked about organizing the data in a few different ways so we could learn more about the types of activities that are your favorites. One person suggested organizing the data into [outdoor] activities and [indoor] activities. Let's try that.

Write "Outdoor Activities" on one self-stick note and "Indoor Activities" on another and post them.

Now, let's sort our data into these two groups.

Place the weekend activity self-stick notes from Session 1.2 under the categories where students decide they belong.

Professional Development

❶ **Dialogue Box:** What's Your Favorite Weekend Activity?, p. 137

Teaching Note

❷ **Save the Charts** Save all charts for the next session.

Students may disagree on where to place certain activities, or they may think some belong in more than one category. For example, students may say that soccer can be played indoors and outdoors. Decide together where to put that piece of data. Students may decide a piece of data belongs more in one category than in another. If they think it belongs equally in both, they may decide to put it between the two categories.

After students sort the data, display a new sheet of chart paper titled "What We Learned," and ask the following questions:

Looking at the data sorted in this way, what do they show us about students' favorite weekend activities? What can we say about them when we organize the data this way?

Write students' observations. They will probably talk about how many more activities there were in one category rather than the other.

> ### What We Learned
>
> Outdoors/Indoors
> > More people like to do outdoor activities.

Sort the data again in a different way, using more than two categories.❶ For example, you could choose the categories of sports, art, TV, reading, and eating. You could also choose a completely different way of looking at the data—such as activities done alone, activities done with family, and activities done with friends. Sort the data accordingly, and then discuss what you can learn from the new organization. Record students' observations on the chart, "What We Learned."❷

> Sports/Reading/Eating/TV/Games
> > Four people's favorite activity was reading
> > and four people's favorite activity was sports.
> > Very few people chose games.

ACTIVITY

Filling Out the "Favorite Things" Questionnaire

20 MIN   INDIVIDUALS

I've prepared a **questionnaire** that uses all of your "Favorite Things" survey questions that you suggested before. We are going to use it to collect responses to your surveys. Each of you will fill out the questionnaire and write your name next to each of your responses so that the people who receive them can ask you questions if something is not clear.

> ### "Favorite Things" Questionnaire
>
> Anita and Darren:
> What's your favorite food?
> Name _____
>
> Carla and Travis:
> What's your favorite animal?
> Name _____
>
> Juanita and Henry:
> What's your favorite game?
> Name _____
>
> Lonzell and Nadia:
> What's your favorite sport?
> Name _____

When you're done, I'll cut the questionnaires into pieces, and each pair will get a response to their survey question from everyone in the class.

Circulate as students complete the survey to make sure that they

- Understand the questions;

- Give clear responses;

- Write their names next to each response.

As students finish, check their questionnaires to make sure that they are complete.

Name _____ Date _____
Pockets, Teeth, and Favorite Things   Daily Practice

Sticker Station Problems

Solve each problem. Show your work.
Write an equation.

NOTE Students use what they know about groups of 10s and 1s to solve story problems.
27, 28, 29

1. Franco went to Sticker Station.
   He bought 2 strips of 10 and 6 singles of frog stickers. He also bought 5 strips of 10 and 7 singles of butterfly stickers. How many stickers did Franco buy?

2. Sally also went to Sticker Station.
   She bought 3 strips of 10 and 5 singles of skateboard stickers. She also bought 4 strips of 10 and 8 singles of snowman stickers. How many stickers did Sally buy?

Session 1.4   Unit 4   5

▲ **Student Activity Book, p. 5**

Math Note

③ Sorting Groups When students played *Guess My Rule* with People in Session 1.1, they dealt with just two groups—those who fit the rule and those who did not. In some cases, the students in the latter category could not be described in any other way. For example, with the rule "wearing a watch," students either are or are not wearing a watch. The group without watches cannot be categorized further. In contrast, the students in the group "not wearing shirts with stripes" could further be described in other categories relating to shirts (shirts with writing, one-color shirts, shirts with designs, and so on).

Name _____ Date _____

Pockets, Teeth, and Favorite Things   Homework

Guess My Rule

Play several games of *Guess My Rule* with a family member or a friend.

NOTE Students have been playing the game "Guess My Rule" with their class. For homework, students play "Guess My Rule" with a family member or a friend. You can play one rule using the circle or with two rules using the Venn diagram.

1. Collect 20 small objects around your home, for example, a pencil, scissors, a paper clip, a stone, a self-stick note, a penny, and other objects.
2. Choose a rule that fits some of the objects.
3. Put two objects that fit your rule in the circle. Put two objects that do **not** fit your rule outside the circle.
4. Your partner does not guess your rule yet. Your partner chooses an object and puts it where he or she thinks it belongs.
5. Tell your partner whether he or she is correct. You should put any misplaced objects where they belong.
6. Repeat steps 4 and 5 until almost all the objects are placed in the circle or outside the circle.
7. Then your partner guesses your rule.
8. Now it is your partner's turn to choose a rule and you play again.

What rules did you use when you played?

1. _____
2. _____
3. _____
4. _____

6   Unit 4   Session 1.4

▲ **Student Activity Book, p. 6**

---

③ Guess My Rule with People: Multiple Categories

25 MIN   CLASS   PAIRS

For the remainder of the session, students play *Guess My Rule* to sort people into two categories. They look more closely at one category and see whether they can further sort people into more specific groups. ③

Briefly play a round of *Guess My Rule* with People. Choose a rule, such as "wearing a striped shirt/not wearing a striped shirt" or "wearing white shoes/not wearing white shoes," that will create a "does not fit the rule" group that students can further separate into more specific categories. Make sure that all the students are sorted into those who fit the rule and those who do not. Record the results.

Today, we found out that [4 people are wearing striped shirts and 18 are not]. This gives us some information about the type of shirt worn by [4] students in our class. But we still don't know much about the shirts worn by students in the other group—just that they are not striped. What are some other categories we could use to further describe their shirts?

List students' ideas. After you decide on the categories, record how many students fit in each one.

Guess My Rule Data: Shirts

Stripes	4
Checks	2
Pictures	2
Writing	5
Pictures and writing	4
Plain	5

Have students work in pairs to make a representation of this set of data. They can use connecting cubes, stick-on dots, self-stick notes, or drawings. If there are some overlapping data, students will have to decide how to show that a piece of data fits into more than one category.

ONGOING ASSESSMENT: Observing Students at Work ✓

Students represent a set of data that has been sorted into multiple categories.

- **Are students able to make a representation that shows all the categories?** Does it clearly show each category?

- **Do students label each category?**

- **If there are overlapping data, how do students represent them?**

Students use connecting cubes to make a representation of the data.

SESSION FOLLOW-UP

4 Daily Practice and Homework

 Daily Practice: For ongoing review, have students complete *Student Activity Book* page 5.

 Homework: Using the directions on *Student Activity Book* page 6, students play *Guess My Rule* at home with a family member or friend using objects they find at home and record the rules they used. Send home copies of Circle for *Guess My Rule* (M45) and Venn Diagram for *Guess My Rule* (M46) to help students sort their objects.

 Student Math Handbook: Students and families may use *Student Math Handbook* pages 105, 106–107, 109 for reference and review. See pages 145–147 in the back of this unit.

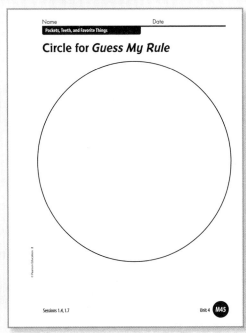

▲ Resource Masters, M45

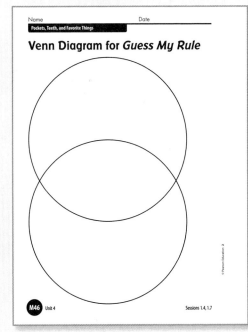

▲ Resource Masters, M46

Organizing "Favorite Things" Data

Math Focus Points

◈ Grouping data into categories based on similar attributes

◈ Describing what the data show about the group surveyed

◈ Sorting the same set of data in different ways

◈ Representing a set of data sorted into categories

Today's Plan			Materials
DISCUSSION **① Describing Favorite Weekend Activity Data**	10 MIN	CLASS	• Self-stick notes; chart: "What's your favorite weekend activity?" (from Session 1.2); chart: "What We Learned" (from Session 1.4)
ACTIVITY **② Organizing Data into Categories**	25 MIN	PAIRS	• "Favorite Things" questionnaire*; self-stick notes, index cards, or small pieces of paper; envelopes; paper clips
ACTIVITY **③ Representing "Favorite Things" Data**	25 MIN	PAIRS	• 12″ x 18″ paper; stick-on dots, self-stick notes, cubes, and other materials for making representations
SESSION FOLLOW-UP **④ Daily Practice**			• *Student Activity Book*, p. 7 • *Student Math Handbook*, pp. 106–107, 109

*See *Materials to Prepare*, p. 23.

Classroom Routines

Today's Number: 12 with Missing Parts Show *Today's Number: 12 with Missing Parts* (T41), which presents several equations with one part missing. The class works together to solve problems such as: _____ + 6 = 12   8 + _____ = 12

12 − 3 = _____   12 = 10 + _____

Focus on one example at a time and ask a few students to explain how they figured out the answer.

DISCUSSION

Describing Favorite Weekend Activity Data

10 MIN   CLASS

Math Focus Points

◆ Grouping data into categories based on similar attributes

◆ Describing what the data show about the group surveyed

Either you or the students think of a way to organize the Favorite Weekend Activity data one last time. Write the new categories on self-stick notes. Sort the data from Session 1.2 as directed by the class.

What can we say about our favorite weekend activities when the data are organized this way?

Add students' observations to the chart, "What We Learned" from Session 1.4.

In what different ways did we organize the weekend activity data? What did you learn about the favorite weekend activities of the students in this class?

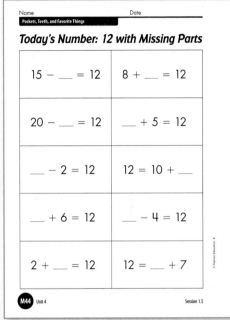

Name _____   Date _____

Pockets, Teeth, and Favorite Things

Today's Number: 12 with Missing Parts

$15 - \_\_ = 12$	$8 + \_\_ = 12$
$20 - \_\_ = 12$	$\_\_ + 5 = 12$
$\_\_ - 2 = 12$	$12 = 10 + \_\_$
$\_\_ + 6 = 12$	$\_\_ - 4 = 12$
$2 + \_\_ = 12$	$12 = \_\_ + 7$

M44   Unit 4   Session 1.5

▲ **Resource Masters, M44; T41**

ACTIVITY

Organizing Data into Categories

25 MIN   PAIRS

Each pair of students will need the set of responses to its "Favorite Things" survey question from Session 1.4, along with some self-stick notes, index cards, or small pieces of paper.

You are going to organize your "Favorite Things" survey responses into categories, as you did with the Favorite Weekend Activity data. You will

• Talk with your partner about ways you might sort the data;

• Try sorting the data in a few ways;

• Choose the way that you think works best.

Later in the lesson, you will make a representation of the sorted data.

Teaching Note

❷ **Clarifying Data** Students will need to decide what to do with responses that they cannot read or that do not answer their question. If responses are unclear, they might ask other students for clarification.

As you move around the classroom, ask students these questions:

- How are you deciding to put your responses into categories?

- What are the names of your categories?

- Why do you think those responses go together?

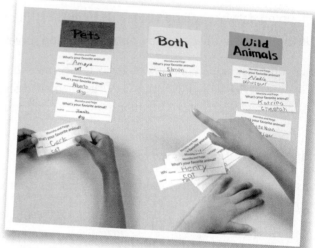

Students sort survey responses into categories.

Encourage students to think of other ways they might organize their data.

Students will need to discuss and then decide what to do with data that fit into more than one or none of their categories.❷ Students may decide to put some data in between categories, make a Venn diagram, or make a category labeled "other" for data that do not fit.

At first, some students may put their data into categories that do not give useful information. For example, they might sort their data by the first letter of each piece. To help students think of more meaningful categories, ask a question such as the following:

What would sorting students' favorite [sports] by the letter that [the sport] begins with tell us about the students in this class?

When students decide on their categories, give them an envelope to store this information and their survey responses. They can use paper clips or other materials to keep their responses in groups.

ONGOING ASSESSMENT: Observing Students at Work

Observe students as they organize a set of data into categories.

- **Can students find similar pieces of data that go together?**

- **Are they able to name the categories they have sorted their data into?**

- **Can they find more than one way to sort the data?**

DIFFERENTIATION: Supporting the Range of Learners

Intervention Some students may find sorting their data into categories challenging. They may need help figuring out how some of their data pieces are similar.

What can you tell me about the kinds of activities students like to do at recess? Which of these responses are similar?

ACTIVITY

25 MIN **PAIRS**

3 Representing "Favorite Things" Data

Pairs begin to make representations of their "Favorite Things" data. Show them the materials they can use.❸

Whatever materials you use, you need to put your data into categories and clearly show the results of your survey so that someone who is not in this class can understand them. Include a title that tells what your question is. Make sure that you label your categories clearly and your names are on your paper.

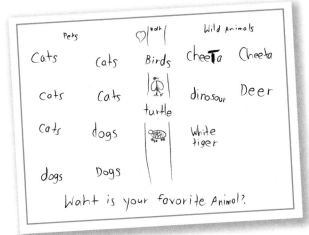

Sample Student Work

Teaching Note

❸ **Practicing Plus 10** As students finish working they should spend a few minutes practicing the Plus 10 combinations, because you will begin to assess students in Session 1.7.

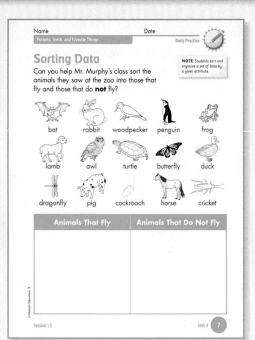

▲ Student Activity Book, p. 7

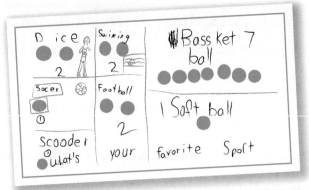

Sample Student Work

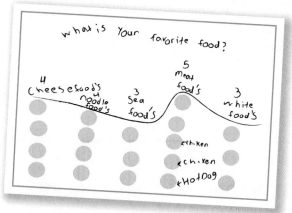

Sample Student Work

ONGOING ASSESSMENT: Observing Students at Work

Observe students as they represent their data and work on communicating clearly the results to their survey.

- **How do students represent the data?** Can they organize them in a picture, table, or graph in a way that shows the data clearly?

- **Do students' representations clearly show their categories?**

SESSION FOLLOW-UP

4 Daily Practice

 Daily Practice: For reinforcement of this unit's content, have students complete *Student Activity Book* page 7.

 Student Math Handbook: Students and families may use *Student Math Handbook* pages 106–107, 109 for reference and review. See pages 145–147 in the back of this unit.

Sharing "Favorite Things" Data

Math Focus Points

- Describing what the data show about the group surveyed
- Using equations to show how the sum of the responses in each category equals the total responses collected
- Interpreting and sharing results from a data investigation

Today's Plan		Materials
ACTIVITY **① Analyzing "Favorite Things" Data**	30 MIN INDIVIDUALS PAIRS	• *Student Activity Book*, p. 8 • Small Yektti Cards • Chart paper with a Venn diagram on it or two yarn loops; "Favorite Things" data representations
DISCUSSION **② Sharing "Favorite Things" Data Results**	30 MIN PAIRS CLASS	• "Favorite Things" data representations
SESSION FOLLOW-UP **③ Daily Practice**		• *Student Activity Book*, p. 9 • *Student Math Handbook*, pp. 106–107, 109, 111

Classroom Routines

What Time is It?: What Time Will it Be? Using The Clock (M43), pairs work together to display 8:30. Display 8:30 on the demonstration clock and ask students *what time it will be* in 30 minutes or one half hour. Ask students to set the new time on their clocks and talk with their partner about what time it will be in half an hour and how they know. Repeat using half hour intervals, varying the start times on the whole and half hours. Remind students of the work they did previously when they figured out that one half hour was also the same as 30 minutes.

Name _____ Date _____

Pockets, Teeth, and Favorite Things

Analyzing Favorite Things Data

Write two things you learned from your Favorite Things survey:

1. _____
_____
_____

2. _____
_____
_____

Write an equation that shows the results of your survey.
_____

How many people answered your survey? _____

How do you know? _____
_____
_____
_____

8 Unit 4   Session 1.6

▲ Student Activity Book, p. 8

Teaching Note

❶ **Limit the Time** Each pair should share for only a few minutes. This sharing time may take more than 30 minutes, depending on how much time you allow each pair.

ACTIVITY
1 Analyzing "Favorite Things" Data

30 MIN INDIVIDUALS PAIRS

Students work individually to analyze the data from their "Favorite Things" survey. They may discuss their thoughts with their partner from the previous session, but students should record their own analysis on *Student Activity Book* page 8.

ONGOING ASSESSMENT: Observing Students at Work

Observe students while they analyze their survey data.

- **Are they able to draw some reasonable conclusions from the data?**

- **Can they write an equation that correctly represents their data?**

- **Are they able to explain how they know how many students responded to the survey?**

DIFFERENTIATION: Supporting the Range of Learners

Extension If students finish their representations and their analysis before the end of the session and you think their work is thorough, they can use the Yekttis cards to play *Guess My Rule* with Two Rules.

DISCUSSION
2 Sharing "Favorite Things" Data Results

30 MIN PAIRS CLASS

Math Focus Points for Discussion

◆ Interpreting and sharing results from a data investigation

Pairs of students share their representations and findings with the class.❶

You and your partner are going to

- Tell the class your survey question;

- Show your representation;

- Tell how you decided on the categories to put your data into;

- Tell what you found out from your survey.

Students share their "Favorite Things" representation.

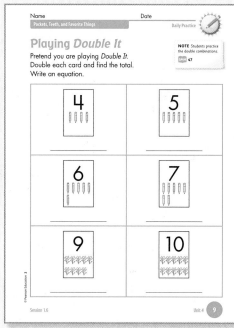

▲ Student Activity Book, p. 9

SESSION FOLLOW-UP

3 Daily Practice

Daily Practice: For ongoing review, have students complete *Student Activity Book* page 9.

Student Math Handbook: Students and families may use *Student Math Handbook* pages 106–107, 109, 111 for reference and review. See pages 145–147 in the back of this unit.

Assessment: Favorite Foods and Plus 10 Combinations

Math Focus Points

◆ Grouping data into categories based on similar attributes

◆ Describing what the data show about the group surveyed

◆ Sorting a set of data by two attributes at one time

◆ Using a Venn diagram to represent a sorted set of data

Today's Plan		Materials
① ACTIVITY **Guess My Rule with Animals**	25 MIN CLASS PAIRS	• *Student Activity Book,* pp. 10–11 • M45*; M46* • Chart paper
② ASSESSMENT ACTIVITY **What's Your Favorite Food? and Plus 10 Combinations**	✓ 35 MIN INDIVIDUALS	• M47–M48*; M51* • Blank paper; scissors
③ SESSION FOLLOW-UP **Daily Practice and Homework**		• *Student Activity Book,* pp. 12–13 • *Student Math Handbook,* pp. 51, 105, 106–107, 108, 109 • M49–M50, Family Letter*

*See *Materials to Prepare,* p. 23.

Classroom Routines

Quick Images: Ten Frames Using Ten-Frame Cards (T28–T29), show two ten-frames, one with 10 dots and one with 8 dots. Follow the basic *Quick Images* activity. Once the class has established the total (28), have students write equations that represent the image. Examples might include: $10 + 10 + 5 + 3 = 28$ or $10 + 10 + 8 = 28$.

Students should be able to explain how their equation represents the ten-frames. Encourage students to look for groups of five and ten. If no one suggests $30 - 2$, challenge students to write an equation using subtraction.

ACTIVITY

Guess My Rule with Animals

25 MIN   CLASS   PAIRS

As a whole class and then in pairs, students play *Guess My Rule* with Animals, first playing with one rule and then with two.

Draw a large circle on a sheet of chart paper or on the board or you can use the transparency, circle for *Guess My Rule* (T42). Using the rule "animals that can fly," write the names of a couple of animals that fit the rule inside the circle. Outside the circle, write the names of a couple of animals that do not fit the rule.❶

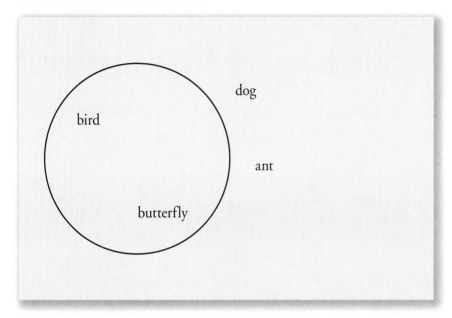

Choose animals with which your students are likely to be familiar. As in other *Guess My Rule* games, students suggest animals that they think either fit or do not fit your rule. Write the names of the animals that fit the rule inside the circle. Write the names of the ones that do not fit the rule outside the circle.

When most students seem to know the rule, have someone guess it. After students have guessed the rule, have them suggest a few more animals to go inside and outside the circle.

Teaching Note

❶ **Preparing for Assessment** *Guess My Rule* with Animals gives students additional experience working with data prior to the assessment they will complete later in the session.

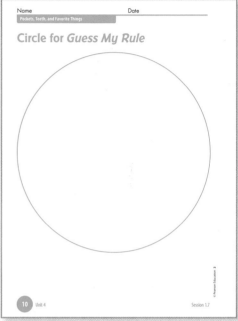

▲ **Student Activity Book, p. 10;**
Resource Masters, M45; T42

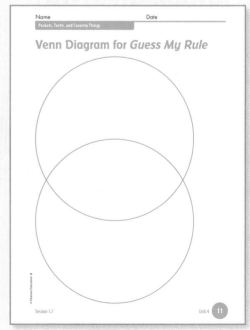

▲ **Student Activity Book, p. 11;**
Resource Masters, M46; T43

Teaching Note

❷ **Venn Diagram** You can also play *Guess My Rule* with three rules using a 3-circle Venn diagram.

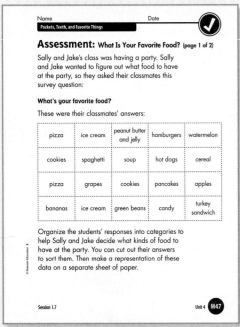

▲ **Resource Masters, M47** *PORTFOLIO*

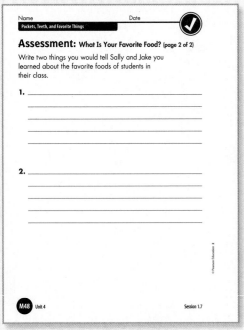

▲ **Resource Masters, M48** *PORTFOLIO*

Play *Guess My Rule* with Animals again, this time with two rules on a Venn diagram or the transparency Venn Diagram for *Guess My Rule* (T43). Choose two new rules, such as "animals with fur" and "pets." Write one animal's name in each circle, one in the overlap, and one outside both circles. Students suggest animals that they think belong in these areas. When many students seem to know the rules, have someone guess them, and again ask students to suggest a few more animals to add to the Venn diagram.

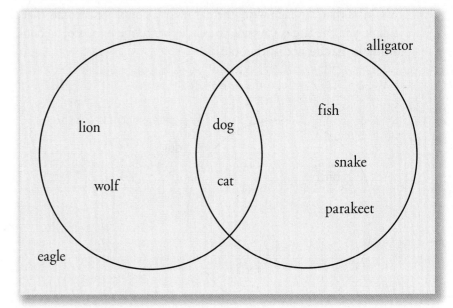

Students play *Guess My Rule* with Animals in pairs. Students play the game using either the circle on *Student Activity Book* page 10 or the Venn diagram on *Student Activity Book* page 11. Have Circle for *Guess My Rule* (M45) and Venn Diagram for *Guess My Rule* (M46) available if pairs wish to play an additional round. ❷

ONGOING ASSESSMENT: Observing Students at Work

As students play *Guess My Rule*, observe how they sort animals by 1 attribute or 2 attributes.

- **Are students able to choose appropriate rules to sort their data sets?**

- **Do students use the data that is already sorted as clues to help them figure out the rule?**

- **Can students identify data that fit both rules and place the data in the appropriate location?**

ASSESSMENT ACTIVITY

What's Your Favorite Food? and Plus 10 Combinations

35 MIN INDIVIDUALS

Professional Development

❸ **Teacher Note:** Assessment: What's Your Favorite Food?, p. 117

❹ **Teacher Note:** Assessing the Plus 10 Combinations, p. 111

Gather the whole class together and tell them that you would like to see how each of them is able to work with organizing and representing data.

Before students begin to work independently on Assessment: What's Your Favorite Food? (M47–M48), read aloud both pages. Students will need a separate sheet of paper to make a representation. They may choose to cut out and sort the "classmates' answers," but they do not have to. Students should be sure to answer the questions on the second page of the assessment. This assessment focuses on sorting data into categories (Benchmark 2) and interpreting a data representation (Benchmark 5).❸

As students finish their representations, begin to assess them on the set of Plus 10 Combinations using their Plus 10 cards. This should take only about one minute per student. This assessment considers students' fluency with the Plus 10 Addition Combinations (Benchmark 7).❹

Record your observations on Assessment Checklist: Plus 10 Combinations (M51). There will be additional opportunities to assess this Benchmark in Investigation 2.

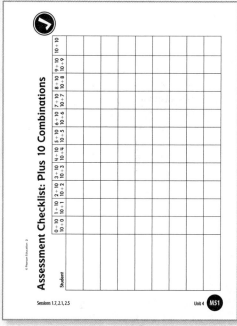

▲ Resource Masters, M51 ✓

ONGOING ASSESSMENT: Observing Students at Work

Observe students as they sort and represent a set of data and answer questions about the data.

- **Can students find similar pieces of data that go together?**

- **Can students name the categories they have sorted their data into?**

- **How do students represent the data?** Can they organize the data clearly in a picture, table, or graph?

- **Do students' representations clearly show their categories?**

- **Are students able to draw some reasonable conclusions from the data?**

Name _____ Date _____
Pockets, Teeth, and Favorite Things   Daily Practice

Even More Sticker Problems

NOTE Students use addition or subtraction to solve 2 story problems.
SMH 79–80

Sticker Station just got a huge delivery! Kira and Jake cannot wait to fill up some of their sticker book pages.

1. Kira has 35 sunshine stickers. How many more does she need to have 50 stickers on the sunshine page in her sticker book?

2. Jake is hoping to fill his puppy page. Right now he has 28 puppy stickers. How many more stickers does he need to have 50 stickers on the puppy page in his sticker book?

12 Unit 4   Session 1.7

© Pearson Education 2

▲ **Student Activity Book, p. 12**

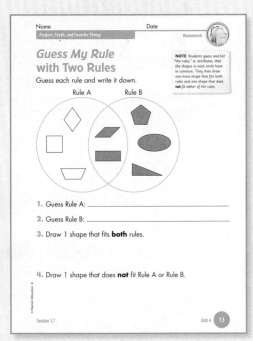

Name _____ Date _____
Pockets, Teeth, and Favorite Things   Homework

Guess My Rule with Two Rules

Guess each rule and write it down.

NOTE Students guess and list "the rules," or attributes, that the shapes in each circle have in common. They then draw one more shape that fits both rules and one shape that does **not** fit either of the rules.

Rule A   Rule B

1. Guess Rule A: _____
2. Guess Rule B: _____
3. Draw 1 shape that fits **both** rules.

4. Draw 1 shape that does **not** fit Rule A or Rule B.

© Pearson Education 2

Session 1.7   Unit 4 13

▲ **Student Activity Book, p. 13**

SESSION FOLLOW-UP

3 Daily Practice and Homework

 Daily Practice: For a review of story problems that focus on finding the difference between one number and 50, have students complete *Student Activity Book* page 12.

Homework: On *Student Activity Book* page 13, students play *Guess My Rule* with Two Rules.

 Student Math Handbook: Students and families may use *Student Math Handbook* pages 51, 105, 106–107, 108, 109 for reference and review. See pages 145–147 in the back of this unit.

Family Letter: Send home copies of the Family Letter (M49–M50).

Mathematical Emphases

Data Analysis Sorting and classifying data

Math Focus Points

◆ Sorting a set of data by two attributes at one time

Data Analysis Representing data

Math Focus Points

◆ Using a Venn diagram to represent a sorted set of data

◆ Ordering, representing, and describing a set of numerical data

◆ Comparing ways of organizing data

◆ Comparing representations of a set of data

◆ Representing data on a line plot

Data Analysis Describing data

Math Focus Points

◆ Describing what the data show about the group surveyed

◆ Interpreting a data representation including a line plot

◆ Describing important features of a data set

◆ Describing a set of numerical data

◆ Comparing two sets of data

◆ Developing a hypothesis based on a set of data

Data Analysis Designing and carrying out a data investigation

Math Focus Points

◆ Making a plan for collecting data

◆ Making predictions about data to be collected

◆ Collecting and recording data from a survey

◆ Interpreting and sharing results from a data investigation

This Investigation also focuses on

◆ Achieving fluency with the Plus 10 combinations
◆ Developing strategies for combining multiple addends

Pocket and Teeth Data

SESSION 2.1 p. 72	Student Activity Book	Student Math Handbook	Professional Development: Read Ahead of Time
Pocket Towers Students collect data about the number of pockets they are wearing. After representing their pocket data with a cube tower, they organize the pocket towers in different ways and describe the information they gather from the pocket-tower representations.	15–17	111	• **Teacher Note:** Describing Numerical Data, p. 122 • **Dialogue Box:** Describing Pocket Data, p. 139
SESSION 2.2 p. 78			
Pocket Data Representations Students compare two different representations of class pocket data, finding the same information in each representation. They describe what the data show them about the number of pockets that students in the class have. Students then calculate the total number of pockets that students are wearing.	18–19	110, 111	• **Teacher Note:** Students' Representations of Numerical Data, p. 124
SESSION 2.3 p. 84			
How Many Teeth Have You Lost? Students compare two representations of the number of teeth lost by students in the class and describe what they can find out from these data representations. Students then make a plan for collecting teeth data from students in other classes.	20–22	111	• **Dialogue Box:** Collecting Data from Other Classrooms, p. 141
SESSION 2.4 p. 89			
Collecting Teeth Data from Other Classes Students make predictions about what they will find out when they collect teeth data from other classes. After a quick review of their data plans, pairs of students go to other classrooms to collect teeth data. The session ends with a short discussion about the experience of collecting data.	20, 22, 23	105	

Classroom Routines See page 16 for an overview.

Quick Images	Today's Number
• T28, Ten-Frame Cards (1–10)	• Overhead coins
• T29, Ten-Frame Cards (Tens)	• M52, *Today's Number: 20 with Missing Parts* Make copies. (1 per student)
• Overhead coins	• T48, *Today's Number*
	• Coin sets (as needed, 4 dimes and 6 pennies per student)

What Time Is It?
- Student clocks, 1 per pair
- Demonstration clock

Materials to Gather	Materials to Prepare
• **Connecting cubes** • **M51, Assessment Checklist: Plus 10 Combinations** ✓ (from Session 1.7)	• **Chart paper** Title a piece of chart paper "Pocket Data." Write students' names in the same order as on the class list. Leave space next to each name to write the number of pockets each student is wearing. • **Class list** Make copies. (1 per student) • **Chart paper** Title a piece of chart paper "Pocket Tower Directions." Write directions on how to create a class set of pocket towers. See example p. 75.
• **Connecting cubes** (about 150) • **Chart paper** • **Self-stick notes** (1 per student) • **Chart: "Pocket Data"** (from Session 2.1) • **Chart paper with self-stick notes**	• **Chart paper** Title a piece of chart paper "Pocket Data 2." Write students' names in the same order as on the class list. Leave space next to each name to write the number of pockets each student is wearing. • **Class list** Make copies. (1 per student)
• **Connecting cubes** (about 150) • **Self-stick notes** (1 per student) • **Chart paper**	• **Notify teachers** Arrange for pairs of your students to visit other classes in a variety of grades to collect data on the number of teeth students have lost. You may have to send more than one pair to each class or arrange for students to collect the data outside math time. • **Class lists** Make a copy of the class list from each class your students will visit. (1 per pair) • **Index cards** Write the teacher's name, the grade, and the room number of each class that your students will visit. (1 per pair) • **Chart paper** Title a piece of chart paper "Teeth We Have Lost."
• **Chart paper** • **Index cards** (1 per pair; from Session 2.3) • **Class lists** (1 per pair; from Session 2.3)	• **Chart paper** Title a sheet of chart paper "Teeth Data from Other Students." List the grade levels from Kindergarten to Grade 5. Leave enough space between each to record the teeth data that students collect. See example p. 90.

Overhead Transparency   ✓ Checklist Available

Pocket and Teeth Data,
continued

	Student Activity Book	Student Math Handbook	Professional Development: Read Ahead of Time	
SESSION 2.5 p. 92				
Representing Teeth Data from Other Classes Pairs of students create their own representations of the teeth data that they collected. They describe what they notice about their own data and then answer questions about the data in other students' representations.	24–26	110, 111		
SESSION 2.6 p. 97				
Comparing Teeth Data Students work in pairs to compare the number of teeth students in another class lost with the number of teeth lost by students in their own class. The class discusses how the teeth data from other classes compare with the teeth data from their own class.	27–29	110, 111	• **Dialogue Box:** Comparing Lost Teeth Data, p. 142	
SESSION 2.7 p. 102				
Mystery Teeth Data Students represent sets of Mystery Teeth Data by using line plots. They then mix up the line plots and try to match them to the unordered Mystery Teeth Data. They make hypotheses about the grade each data set represents.	31–33	110, 111	• **Dialogue Box:** Discussing Mystery Data, p. 144	
SESSION 2.8 p. 108				
End-of-Unit Assessment As a class, students collect data about how many books they read in a week. Using these data, students work on assessment tasks focused on organizing, representing, describing, and comparing sets of data.	34	108, 110, 111	• **Teacher Note:** End-of-Unit Assessment, p. 126	

Materials to Gather	Materials to Prepare
• **M51, Assessment: Plus 10 Combinations** (from Session 1.7) ☑ • **Class lists with teeth data** (from Session 2.4) • **12″ x 18″ paper** (1 sheet per pair) • **Markers, self-stick notes, stick-on dots, cubes, tiles, stamps, and other materials for making representations** (as needed)	
• **Teeth-data representations from other classrooms** (1 per pair; from Session 2.5) • **Self-stick note graph** (from Session 2.3) • **Chart paper**	• **Teeth-data line plot** Use the graph of stick-on notes you saved from Session 2.3 to create a line plot of the teeth data from your own class on an $8^{1}/_{2}″$ x 11″ sheet of paper. Make copies. (1 per student)
• **Teeth data from other class** (1 per class; from Session 2.5)	• **M53–M56, Mystery Teeth Data, Class A–D** Make copies. (1 of 4 sheets per student) • **Chart paper** Label chart paper with one title per sheet as follows: "Class A," "Class B," "Class C," and "Class D." (4 sheets)
	• **M57–M59, End-of-Unit Assessment** Make copies. (1 per student) • **Class list** Make copies. (1 per student)

☑ Checklist Available

Pocket Towers

Math Focus Points

◆ Ordering and representing a set of numerical data

◆ Interpreting a data representation including a line plot

◆ Describing important features of a set of data

◆ Comparing ways of organizing data

Vocabulary

mode

Today's Plan		Materials
ACTIVITY **①** **Introducing How Many Pockets** 20 MIN CLASS		• Connecting cubes (5–10 per student); chart: "Pocket Data"*
ACTIVITY **②** **Organizing Pocket Towers** 25 MIN CLASS GROUPS		• *Student Activity Book,* p. 15 • M51 (from Session 1.7) ☑ • Connecting cubes (50–100 per group); class list (1 per group)*; chart: "Pocket Data" (from previous activity); chart: "Pocket Tower Directions" (1 sheet)
DISCUSSION **③** **Pocket Towers** 15 MIN CLASS		• Pocket-tower representations (3 or 4 sets; from previous activity)
SESSION FOLLOW-UP **④** **Daily Practice**		• *Student Activity Book,* pp. 16–17 • *Student Math Handbook,* p. 111

*See *Materials to Prepare,* p. 69.

Classroom Routines

Today's Number: 20 with Missing Parts Each student completes *Today's Number: 20 with Missing Parts* (M52). When they have finished, pairs compare answers. Select a couple of examples to discuss as a class.

ACTIVITY

1 Introducing How Many Pockets

20 MIN CLASS

I am going to collect pocket data from the whole class. The activities we are about to do are similar to the ones we did in the pocket routine, but instead of focusing on the total number of pockets, we'll be focusing on how many *students* are wearing certain numbers of pockets. ❶

Each student makes a tower of cubes that shows how many pockets he or she is wearing. For example, a student wearing 4 pockets would make a tower of 4 cubes. ❷

Post the "Pocket Data" chart and ask students to bring their towers to a central location, perhaps lined up on the edge of the board. As students bring up their towers, record their number of pockets next to their names on the chart. Do not order the cube towers in any way.

Students create cube towers that show how many pockets they are wearing.

When all the towers have been collected, ask students to think about the correspondence between the number of students and the number of towers.

We collected data from the 15 students in our class. Should we have 15 towers? Why or why not?

The number of towers may not be the same as the number of students because some students may have zero pockets. Remind students how they decided to handle this situation. As a group, count the towers, and then determine the number of people who have zero pockets.

Professional Development

❶ **Teacher Note:** Describing Numerical Data, p. 122

Teaching Note

❷ **Zero Pockets** You will probably encounter the issue of how to represent zero pockets. It is difficult to think of a tower with zero cubes, but it is important to know how many people have zero pockets. Resolving this will probably involve a short discussion. Some classes have used self-stick notes to keep track of the number of people with zero pockets.

Name		Date	
Pockets, Teeth, and Favorite Things			

Today's Number: 20 with Missing Parts

15 + __ = 20	35 − __ = 20
50 − __ = 20	__ + 5 = 20
55 − __ = 20	10 + __ = 20
__ + 0 = 20	45 − __ = 20
25 − __ = 20	__ − 15 = 20

M52 Unit 4   Session 2.1

▲ **Resource Masters, M52**

❸ **People vs. Pockets** At this point, students will not always accurately distinguish between the number of people who have [3] pockets and the number of pockets. Students will work on this distinction throughout this Investigation.

❹ **Organizing for a Purpose** Students may make suggestions for organizing the data that would not be helpful for gathering information (e.g., "Put towers together that would make 10"). If this happens, remind them of the purpose of organizing the data.

Name _____ Date _____

Pockets, Teeth, and Favorite Things

Pocket Data from Our Class

Look at the pocket towers you have organized and use them to answer the questions.

1. How many people were wearing 4 pockets? _____

2. What is the most pockets that students had on their clothes today? _____ How many people had this number of pockets? _____

3. What is the fewest pockets that students had on their clothes today? _____ How many people had this number of pockets? _____

4. Circle which is more:
   Number of people wearing 6 pockets   **OR**   Number of people wearing 7 pockets

5. How many pockets did you have on your clothes? _____

6. How many people in the class had more pockets than you did? _____

7. How many people in the class had fewer pockets than you did? _____

8. How many people in the class had the same number of pockets as you did? _____

Session 2.1   Unit 4   **15**

▲ **Student Activity Book, p. 15**

Ask students questions to help them distinguish between the number of people and the number of pockets.❸ For example:

What does this tower of 4 cubes show?

What does each cube stand for?

~~What does each tower stand for?~~

How many people have 2 pockets?

How many people have zero pockets?

25 MIN   CLASS   GROUPS

ACTIVITY

❷ Organizing Pocket Towers

We were able to gather some information about the number of pockets students are wearing today, but we could learn more if we organized the towers in some way. How could we organize the pocket towers to find out more about the number of pockets people are wearing today?

Ask students to think about which towers go together and how to put the towers in order. Listen to students' ideas and encourage them to think about both grouping and ordering.❹ They will have time to experiment with their ideas as they work in groups.

Students work in groups of 3 or 4 to create and organize their own set of pocket towers. Each group will need connecting cubes, a class list, and *Student Activity Book* page 15.

Work with your group to make a class set of pocket towers to match the set we have here. (Point to the pocket towers on the edge of the board.) You can use the "Pocket Data" chart to help you build your set. Copy the information from the chart onto the class list. How many towers do you think you should have when you're done building?

When you have completed your set of pocket towers, organize them in a few different ways, and then choose one that you might share with the class.

Post the directions you prepared ahead of time and read them together.

> ### Pocket Tower Directions
>
> 1. Make a class set of pocket towers.
>
> 2. Check to make sure that you have everyone's data.
>
> 3. Organize the pocket towers.
>
> 4. Make sure that you show kids who have zero pockets.
>
> 5. Answer the questions on *Student Activity Book* page 15.

You may find that it is a good time to continue the Plus 10 combinations assessment with some students during this activity. Record your observations on Assessment Checklist: Plus 10 Combinations (M51).

ONGOING ASSESSMENT: Observing Students at Work

Observe students as they organize and order a set of data and describe information they gathered from the data.

- **How do students represent the people with zero pockets?**

- **Do students group the data?** Do students put the data in an order?

- **Do students understand that each tower represents the number of pockets worn by one person?**

- **Are students able to use their organized towers to answer the questions?**

- **Do students know what aspect of this representation tells them the number of pockets and what aspect tells them the number of people?**

Identify two or three groups that have organized the towers differently to share their organization during the discussion. Choose one group that orders the towers from least to greatest.

Professional Development
⑤ **Dialogue Box:** Describing Pocket Data, p. 139

DISCUSSION

③ Pocket Towers

15 MIN   CLASS

Math Focus Points for Discussion

◆ Comparing ways of organizing data

◆ Interpreting a representation of numerical data

Prior to the discussion, ask the two or three groups you have identified to save their cube towers. Have the other students return their cubes to the storage containers.

I saw students organizing their towers in a few different ways. Let's have group [1] describe how you organized your towers.⑤

Ask one student from each group you have identified to describe his or her group's organization of pocket towers. Students are likely to group towers of the same height together.

These three groups organized the towers in different ways. Those of you who arranged the towers in the same way as group [1], raise your hands. If you arranged the towers like group [2], raise your hands. What about group [3]?

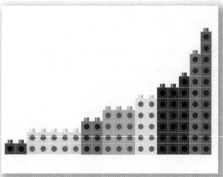

Discuss anything students notice about a particular arrangement of towers. As you look at each way of organizing the pocket towers, ask students to compare how one way is the same as or different from another. For example, ask students to compare a representation in which the set of towers is grouped but unordered with another representation in which the towers are grouped and ordered from least to greatest. Students are likely to notice that it is easier to describe and compare features of the data when the towers are grouped and organized in some way.

Focus the next part of the discussion on the set of towers that has been grouped and ordered.

Look carefully at this group of towers that are organized from shortest to tallest. Now what can we tell about the number of pockets students wore today? What do you notice?

As students share what they notice, help them relate their observations to what the information tells them about the class. For example, if a student says, "There are the most [2]s," ask questions such as these:

- What does that tell us about the number of pockets students wore today?
- What do those towers of [2] cubes stand for?
- How many towers of [2] are there?
- What does that tell us?

After students share their observations, focus on some of the features of the data that students have not brought up.

What is the greatest number of pockets students wore today? What is the fewest number? The number of pockets students in this class are wearing today ranges from [0] to [11]. What is the most common number of pockets students have today? This is called the mode in this set of data.

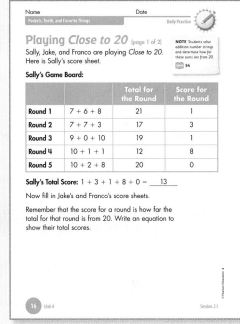

▲ Student Activity Book, p. 16

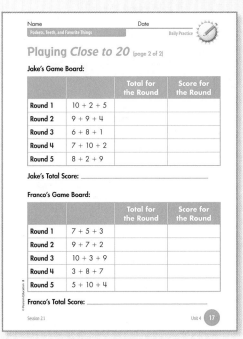

▲ Student Activity Book, p. 17

 SESSION FOLLOW-UP
Daily Practice

 Daily Practice: For ongoing review, have students complete *Student Activity Book* pages 16–17.

 Student Math Handbook: Students and families may use *Student Math Handbook* page 111 for reference and review. See pages 145–147 in the back of this unit.

Pocket Data Representations

Math Focus Points

◈ Comparing representations of a set of data

◈ Ordering, representing, and describing a set of numerical data

◈ Interpreting a data representation including a line plot

◈ Developing strategies for combining multiple addends

Vocabulary
outlier
line plot

Today's Plan		Materials
ACTIVITY ❶ Pocket Towers and Pocket Plot	25 MIN · CLASS	• Connecting cubes (about 150); chart: "Pocket Data 2"; self-stick notes (1 per student)
ACTIVITY ❷ How Many Pockets Altogether?	20 MIN · CLASS · INDIVIDUALS	• Class list (1 per student)*; chart: "Pocket Data 2" (from Activity 1)
ACTIVITY ❸ Introducing Line Plot	15 MIN · CLASS	• *Student Activity Book,* p. 18 • Chart paper with self-stick notes (from Activity 1)
SESSION FOLLOW-UP ❹ Daily Practice and Homework		• *Student Activity Book,* pp. 18–19 • *Student Math Handbook,* pp. 110, 111

*See *Materials to Prepare,* p. 69.

Classroom Routines

What Time Is It?: What Time Will It Be? Write 10:30 on the board. Ask students to set their clocks to that time. Then ask,

In 30 minutes, or one half hour, what time will it be?

Ask students to set the new time on their clocks and talk with their partner about what time it will be and how they know. Then ask them how that time would look on a digital clock (11:00). Repeat using half-hour intervals, varying the start times on the whole and half hours. Remind students of the work they did previously when they figured out that one half hour was the same as 30 minutes.

ACTIVITY

Pocket Towers and Pocket Plot

25 MIN   CLASS

Again, students are going to collect data on how many pockets they have. Then they will make some predictions.

What predictions do you have about this data we're about to collect? How do you think the data may be different from the pocket data in our last session?

After students make predictions, they make towers of how many pockets they are wearing today. This time, they should also write their number of pockets on a self-stick note and put it on their towers.

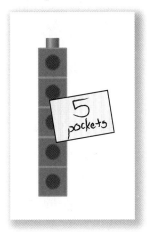

On the "Pocket Data 2" chart, record each student's pocket data. You will use this chart in the next activity.

Put the towers in a central place and ask the students to suggest a way of organizing the towers. Choose a way to organize the towers so that towers of the same number of cubes are grouped together. After you arrange the data, ask students what they notice.

Next, make a graph using the self-stick notes on which students wrote their number of pockets.❶ Arrange the notes on a piece of chart paper, putting the same number of pockets together and putting the numbers in order. As you arrange them, explain what you are doing.❷

I am putting the "1 pockets" together, the "3 pockets" together, and so on, just like when we arranged the towers. This way you can see how many students in the class have each number of pockets.

Math Note

❶ **Case Value and Frequency** The cube towers and self-stick note graph are two different types of representations of the same data set. The towers represent each individual pocket within each piece of data and each self-stick note represents a set of pockets. The first is a case-value representation, the second is a frequency representation.

Professional Development

❷ **Teacher Note:** Students' Representations of Numerical Data, p. 124

Teaching Note

❸ **Many-to-One Relationships** It is important for students to recognize the "many-to-one" relationship of the cube towers and the self-stick notes. That is, each self-stick note represents a different tower. A tower and a note both represent the number of pockets 1 student has.

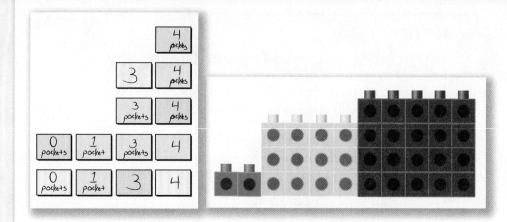

When the self-stick notes are organized, ask students questions to help them understand this new representation.

What does each self-stick note stand for?

What does the number on each note stand for?

How many people did we collect data from? How can you tell?

What does this note tell us? [Point to one note.]

Then shift students' focus to important features of the data and what they can learn from these representations.

We have two representations of the same information or data. The graph of self-stick notes shows how many people are wearing each number of pockets. The pocket towers show how many pockets each person has; you can see each pocket. Looking at these two representations of the pocket data, what can you say about the number of pockets students in the class are wearing today?

Students now can look at two types of representations of the same set of data. As students share their observations about what they notice in one representation, ask students to find that same information in the other representation.❸

Simon says that he can see that there are 5 people who have 4 pockets on the notes graph. Can someone show us that 5 people have 4 pockets in the towers?

After students share their observations, focus on some of the features of the data that students have not brought up.

What is the greatest number of pockets students are wearing today?

What is the fewest number of pockets students are wearing today?

What is the most common number of pockets students are wearing today? (That's the mode.)

Is there any unusual data—a number far away from the rest? That's called an outlier.

ONGOING ASSESSMENT: Observing Students at Work

- **How do students describe each representation?** Can they identify greatest, fewest, and most common number of pockets?

- **How do students compare the two representations?** Can they identify the same data in each set?

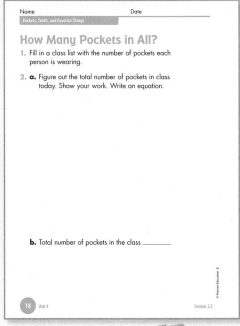

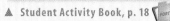
▲ **Student Activity Book, p. 18**

ACTIVITY

2 How Many Pockets Altogether?

20 MIN | CLASS | INDIVIDUALS

Students begin working on *Student Activity Book* page 18 in class. They will finish the problem for homework.

Now, you are going to figure out the total number of pockets the class is wearing today.

Hand out a class list to each student. Read aloud from the "Pocket Data" chart. Students should record the number of pockets for each student on the list as you read them aloud.

You now have a class list that shows how many pockets students are wearing today. What could we do to find out the total number of pockets students are wearing today?

Students might say:

"We could add up all the numbers."

[Anita] suggested adding up all the numbers. We have many numbers. Can anyone suggest some strategies that might make it easier to add all these numbers?

Are there numbers I might add together first?

What numbers would be easiest to add together first?

How can I keep track of the numbers I have already added?

Professional Development

④ **Teacher Note:** Describing Numerical Data, p. 122

After you have discussed a few different strategies for approaching this problem, give each student a blank sheet of paper to find the total. Students should work on this problem for only 20 minutes and then finish it for homework, showing their final work on *Student Activity Book* page 18.

ONGOING ASSESSMENT: Observing Students at Work

Observe students as they use strategies to find the total number of pockets in the class.

- **Do students choose reasonable strategies for combining the quantities?**

- **What strategies do students use?** Do they combine quantities that make 10? Do they combine doubles? Do they use combinations they know?

- **Are students able to keep track of the numbers they have already combined and those they still need to combine?**

DIFFERENTIATION: Supporting the Range of Learners

Intervention Some students may be overwhelmed by the quantity of numbers they need to add. You may need to help them develop a system for choosing numbers to add together while keeping track of the ones they have already added. Begin by asking students whether there are any 2 numbers they could easily add together, or ask them to identify pairs of numbers that make 10. Suggest crossing out the numbers as they are used.

Extension Students who finish early can calculate the total number of pockets from today's pocket data collection and compare it with yesterday's total.

ACTIVITY

15 MIN   CLASS

3 Introducing Line Plots

We are going to make one more representation of the pocket data we collected today. This representation is called a line plot.④ As we make the line plot, think about how it is similar to our pocket towers and plot of self-stick notes and how it is different.

Now, can you help me figure out the fewest and greatest number of pockets in the class today? This information will help me make a line plot.

Draw a line on the board. Put the least value at the left end of the line and the greatest value at the right end and then fill in the numbers at equal intervals. Under the numbers write "Number of Pockets" and explain this label.

Now we'll put Xs on the line plot to show how many pockets each of us have. Let's use the data from our self-stick notes to remind us how many pockets each of us has.

Have one student read aloud from the graph of self-stick notes how many pockets each student has. As each number is read, place an X above that number on the line plot.

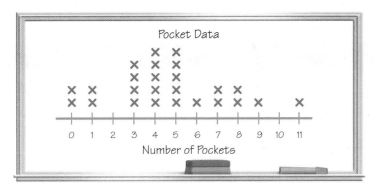

Each of these Xs represents a person. How many Xs do you think there should be? Why do you think there should be that many?

After students share how many Xs they think there should be, count them.

How should the number of Xs compare with the number of towers or the number of self-stick notes?

Compare the number of Xs with the number of cube towers and self-stick notes. There should be the same number of notes, but there may be fewer towers if there are students with zero pockets. ⑤

SESSION FOLLOW-UP

Daily Practice and Homework

 Daily Practice: For ongoing review, have students complete *Student Activity Book* page 19.

 Homework: Students finish *Student Activity Book* page 18. They will need to use the class list with the numbers of pockets recorded on it to complete the homework.

 Student Math Handbook: Students and families may use *Student Math Handbook* pages 110 and 111 for reference and review. See pages 145–147 in the back of this unit.

Teaching Note

⑤ **Preparing for Session 2.4** If you have not already done so, make plans for how your students will collect teeth data from other classrooms. See Investigation Planner, p. 69.

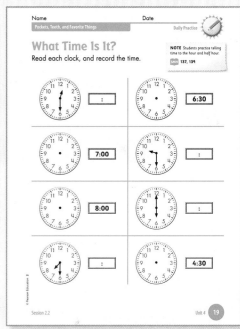

▲ **Student Activity Book, p. 19**

How Many Teeth Have You Lost?

Math Focus Points

◆ Comparing representations of a set of data

◆ Describing what the data show about the group surveyed

◆ Making a plan for collecting data

Today's Plan			Materials
DISCUSSION ① **Comparing Teeth Representations**	🕐 25 MIN	👥 CLASS	• Connecting cubes; self-stick notes; chart: "Teeth We Have Lost"*
ACTIVITY ② **Making a Plan**	🕐 35 MIN	👥 PAIRS	• *Student Activity Book*, p. 20 • Index cards*; class lists*
SESSION FOLLOW-UP ③ **Daily Practice and Homework**			• *Student Activity Book*, pp. 21–22 • *Student Math Handbook*, p. 111

*See *Materials to Prepare*, p. 69.

Classroom Routines

Quick Images: Ten-Frames Using Ten Frame Cards (T28–T29), show four ten-frames, three with 10 dots and one with 6 dots. Follow the basic *Quick Images* activity. Once the class has established the total amount (36), have students write equations that represent the image. Examples might include: $10 + 10 + 10 + 5 + 1 = 36$ or $10 + 10 + 10 + 6 = 36$. Students should be able to explain how their equation represents the ten-frames. Encourage students to look for groups of five and ten. If no one suggests $40 - 4 = 36$, challenge students to write an equation using subtraction.

DISCUSSION

Comparing Teeth Representations

25 MIN   **CLASS**

Math Focus Points for Discussion

◆ Comparing representations of a set of data

◆ Describing what the data show about the group surveyed

Begin by talking briefly about the experience of losing teeth and letting students know that you are going to take a survey of the number of teeth that they have lost.❶ Distribute cubes for making towers.

Today, you are going to build a tower of the number of teeth you have lost.

As they do this, distribute self-stick notes and have students write the number of teeth they have lost on them. Have students attach the notes to their towers. Students who have not yet lost any teeth will not have a tooth tower, but they should make a self-stick note that shows their data.

Now that your towers are done, we need to arrange them in order so that all of you can see how many people lost each number of teeth.

Ask one student to arrange the towers on the edge of the board and ask another to take off the self-stick notes and arrange them into a graph on the board, as you did with the pocket data.❷

Teaching Notes

❶ **Be Sensitive** Note that tooth loss might be a sensitive subject for some second graders, especially if they have not yet lost a tooth. Prior to collecting data, acknowledge that not all second graders have lost a tooth or that some older students may have lost several teeth. Allow these students to share that information if they want to.

❷ **Save the Plot** At the end of the session, save the self-stick note graph for use in Session 2.6. Transfer data to a line plot. Make a copy for each student to use in Session 2.6.

❸ **Many-to-One Relationships** It is important for students to recognize the "many-to-one" relationship of the cube towers to self-stick notes. Each self-stick note represents a different tower. A tower and a note both represent the number of teeth lost by one child.

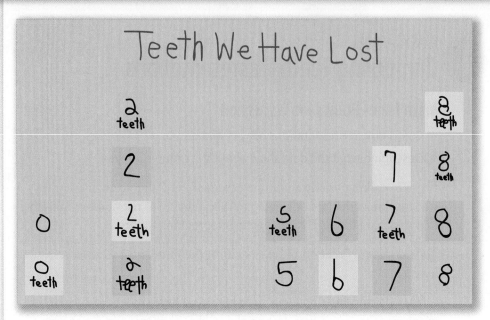

Looking at our two representations, what can you say about the number of teeth lost by students in our classroom?

Students might say:

"Four people have lost 2 teeth."

Students are likely to focus on how many people have lost different numbers of teeth. As they do this, ask them to point out where they found that information in one of the representations. Then ask them to find that information in the other representation.

[Lonzell] noticed that four people have lost two teeth. Let's check the teeth towers. How many towers of 2 cubes do you think there should be? Can someone show us?

For each observation that a student makes about one representation, ask whether he or she can see that same information in the other representation.

Some information will be represented on the graph but not in the teeth towers.❸ Zero teeth may be recorded on the self-stick notes but will not be shown with the cubes. You might ask all of the students who have lost zero teeth to stand up or raise their hands so that they can be compared with the number of self-stick notes.

If we visited another second-grade class, what do you think the data would look like? The same as ours? Different from ours? Why?

ACTIVITY

35 MIN   PAIRS

② Making a Plan

Today, we collected information about the number of teeth lost by students in this class. During the next few days you are going to be finding out about the number of teeth lost by students in other classes. You will collect the data, organize it, and then represent it in some way.❹❺

Organize students in pairs. Depending on the number of students in your class and the number of classes in your school, you may need to assign two pairs to the same class; they can compare their data and representations. Assign classrooms by distributing index cards that list the teacher's name, the grade, and room number. Then distribute the corresponding class lists.

Before you go to collect data from other classes, you need to plan how you will do it. Think about how you will:

• Tell the students what you are doing;

• Record the students' answers;

• Make sure that you have asked everyone your question.

Look together at *Student Activity Book* page 20. Ask students about each question and the decisions they might make.

When you go into the other classroom, what might you say to the group to explain what you are doing? How would you say it differently if you are going into a kindergarten classroom or a fifth-grade classroom?

Students should try out some different ways of presenting their survey to the classrooms they will visit.❺

It will be important for you to keep track of the answers people give you. How might you record students' answers?

Explain to students that they need to think about each of these parts for collecting their data, discuss their ideas with their partner, and then write down what they decide to do. Point out that they also need to explain in writing how they will make sure that they have asked everyone.

Name _____ Date _____

Pockets, Teeth, and Favorite Things

Our Plan for Collecting Data ✏

Discuss these questions with your partner.
Record your answers.

1. What class will you collect data from?
   _____

2. What will you say to the class to introduce your survey?
   _____
   _____
   _____

3. What question will you ask?
   _____
   _____

4. How will you keep track of people's answers?
   _____
   _____

5. How will you make sure you ask everyone the question?
   _____
   _____

20 Unit 4   Session 2.3

▲ Student Activity Book, p. 20

Teaching Notes

❹ **Tell the Teachers** Remind teachers in other classrooms that your students will be coming tomorrow to collect teeth data.

❺ **How Many Teeth Overall** Students in other classrooms may not be sure whether they are being asked how many teeth they have lost this year or overall. Ask your students to think about how they can make it clear that they want to know how many teeth students have lost overall.

Differentiation

❻ **English Language Learners** You may want to meet with English Language Learners in a small group to review these instructions and to allow them to practice asking the question, **How many teeth have you lost?** Begin by asking each student the question yourself. Then have each student ask another student the question. You can also help English Language Learners represent their data in a simple line plot and practice interpreting it in preparation for the *End-of-Unit Assessment*.

Professional Development

7 Dialogue Box: Collecting Data from Other Classrooms, p. 141

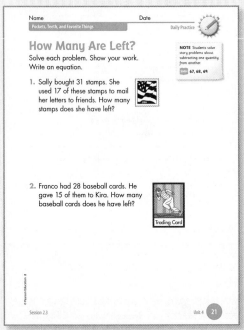

▲ Student Activity Book, p. 21

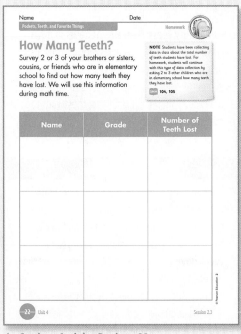

▲ Student Activity Book, p. 22

As pairs work, ask them to explain to you what they are going to do when they visit the other classroom. **7**

Students plan how to collect their data.

ONGOING ASSESSMENT: Observing Students at Work

Observe students as they think through how they will present the project, plan how to collect data and record responses, and determine how to make sure that everyone answers the question.

- **Can they choose an appropriate way to record the data they collect?**

- **What ways do they come up with to make sure that everyone answers the survey?**

SESSION FOLLOW-UP

3 Daily Practice and Homework

 Daily Practice: For ongoing review, have students complete *Student Activity Book* page 21.

 Homework: Students survey their brothers, sisters, cousins, or friends who are in elementary school about how many teeth they have lost. They record their data on *Student Activity Book* page 22. They will use this data in a discussion in Session 2.4.

 Student Math Handbook: Students and families may use *Student Math Handbook* page 111 for reference and review. See pages 145–147 in the back of this unit.

Collecting Teeth Data from Other Classes

Math Focus Points

◆ Making predictions about data to be collected

◆ Collecting and recording data from a survey

Today's Plan		Materials
DISCUSSION ① **Predictions About Teeth Data**	15 MIN CLASS	• *Student Activity Book*, p. 22 (from Session 2.3) • Chart: "Teeth Data from Other Students"
ACTIVITY ② **Collecting Teeth Data from Other Classes**	45 MIN PAIRS CLASS	• *Student Activity Book*, p. 20 (from Session 2.3) • Index cards (from Session 2.3); class lists (from Session 2.3)
SESSION FOLLOW-UP ③ **Daily Practice**		• *Student Activity Book*, p. 23 • *Student Math Handbook*, p. 105

Classroom Routines

Today's Number: 42 Using Dimes and Pennies Students use pennies and dimes to make 42. Challenge them to find all possible combinations. Post the combinations and discuss what students notice, paying particular attention to how the number of pennies decreases by 10 when a dime is added.

❶ **Save the Predictions** Record students' predictions on a sheet of chart paper and save them for Session 2.6.

DISCUSSION

Predictions About Teeth Data

15 MIN   CLASS

Math Focus Points for Discussion

◆ Making predictions about data to be collected

Students will need their completed homework on *Student Activity Book* page 22 for this discussion. Post the "Teeth Data from Other Students" chart to organize and record the tooth-loss data that they collected.

Teeth Data from Other Students	
Kindergarten	Grade 1
Grade 2	Grade 3
Grade 4	Grade 5

Did anyone collect data from a kindergartener? How many teeth did that kindergartener lose? Did anyone else collect data from a kindergartener?

Record all the data about kindergarteners on the chart. Ask the same question and record the data in the same way for each grade level. This should not take more than a few minutes.

Today you are going to collect data from other classes about how many teeth students have lost. Let's make some predictions about what you will find out.❶ The data you and your classmates collected for homework might help you make a prediction.

What do you think the data that you collect will look like? What will it look like from younger classes? From older classes? From other second-grade classes? Why?

ACTIVITY

45 MIN PAIRS CLASS

② Collecting Teeth Data from Other Classes

Before students go to the other classrooms, ask them to review *Student Activity Book* page 20, and gather their index cards, class lists, and other materials. Remind them to be respectful to the students whom they survey.

Gathering the data should not take a long time. Each teacher is expecting you. After you have collected all of your data, you and your partner should come back to our classroom and start to think about how you might organize and represent your data.

After everyone has returned from collecting their data, have a short discussion about this experience. ②

- Did the data gathering go the way you expected?

- What was different from what you expected?

- Did anything interesting or surprising come up as you collected the data?

- How did you know when you had collected data from every person and that you didn't collect data from the same person twice?

Students will probably be eager to share their experiences in data gathering. Be sure to address any questions they have about methods for systematically collecting, recording, and keeping track of data. Explain that they will be organizing and representing their data in the next session.

SESSION FOLLOW-UP

③ Daily Practice

 Daily Practice: For reinforcement of this unit's content, have students complete *Student Activity Book* page 23.

 Student Math Handbook: Students and families may use *Student Math Handbook* page 105 for reference and review. See pages 145–147 in the back of this unit.

Teaching Note

② **Play While You Wait** If you have to wait for a few students to return, you might choose to play a round of *Guess My Rule* with People, using 2 rules.

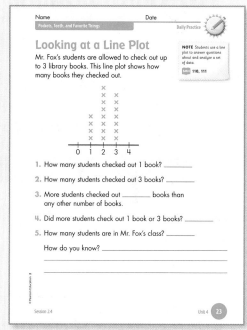

▲ Student Activity Book, p. 23

Representing Teeth Data from Other Classes

Math Focus Points

◆ Ordering, representing, and describing a set of numerical data

◆ Interpreting a data representation including a line plot

◆ Interpreting and sharing results from a data investigation

Today's Plan		Materials
① ACTIVITY **Representing Teeth Data from Other Classes**	🕐 👪 👫 40 MIN CLASS PAIRS	• M51 (from Session 1.7) ☑️ • Class lists with teeth data (from Session 2.4); 12″ x 18″ paper; markers, self-stick notes, stick-on dots, cubes, tiles, stamps, and other materials for making representations
② ACTIVITY **Describing Teeth Data**	🕐 👫 20 MIN PAIRS	• *Student Activity Book,* p. 24 • *Student Activity Book,* p. 25
③ SESSION FOLLOW-UP **Daily Practice**		• *Student Activity Book,* p. 26 • *Student Math Handbook,* pp. 110, 111

Classroom Routines

What Time Is It? What Time Will It Be? Write 2:00 on the board and ask pairs to set their clocks to that time. Then, introduce students to the quarter hour by asking What would the clock look like if the minute hand only went 15 minutes past 2:00? Write 2:15 on the board.

Does anyone know what time this is? This time is 2:15 or 15 minutes past 2:00.

On the demonstration clock, move the minute hand 15 minutes counting by ones as you go. Highlight that the hour hand is slightly past the 2, indicating that it is not exactly 2:00, but some minutes past 2:00. Repeat with 1:00, 6:00 and 12:00. Students work in pairs setting their clocks to 15 minutes past the hour and writing the new time in digital notation.

ACTIVITY

Representing Teeth Data from Other Classes

40 MIN   CLASS   PAIRS

Today, you and your partner are going to make a representation of the teeth data that you collected from another class. You and your partner will need to decide how to organize the data and how to represent them.

Each of your representations should include a title that tells the grade level of the students that you surveyed and the question that you asked. You should also check to make sure that your representation includes all your data.

Remind students of the types of representations they have made so far during this unit. Brainstorm together some other ways to display the teeth data.

- How could you use dots, drawings, or other materials to represent the number of teeth students in another classroom lost?❶

- How could you use pictures or graphs to show what you found out?

Teaching Note

❶ **Make It Permanent** If students decide to use cubes or tiles, then they need to make a permanent representation on paper, as well.

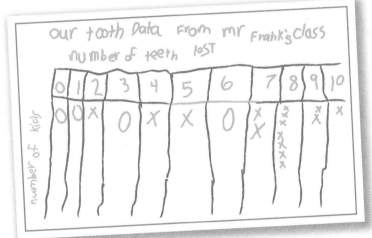

Sample Student Work

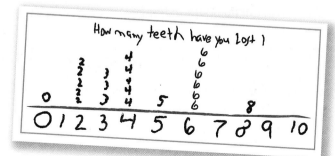

Sample Student Work

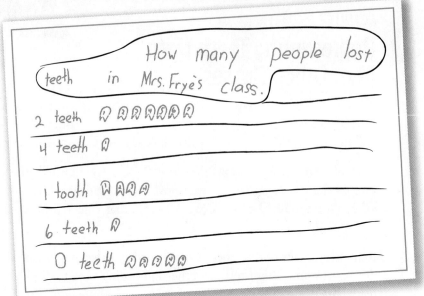

How many people lost teeth in Mrs. Frye's class.

2 teeth 🦷🦷🦷🦷🦷🦷

4 teeth 🦷

1 tooth 🦷🦷🦷🦷

6 teeth 🦷

0 teeth 🦷🦷🦷🦷🦷

Sample Student Work

You may find that it is a good time to continue the +10 combinations assessment with some students during this activity. Record your observations on Assessment Checklist: Plus 10 Combinations (M51).

ONGOING ASSESSMENT: Observing Students at Work

Observe students as they organize and represent the data they collected in a way that clearly communicates what they found out.

- **How are students keeping track of the data they are representing?** Do they check to see whether everyone's data are represented?

- **How have students chosen to represent the data?** Do they show each individual tooth in a way similar to the teeth towers, or do they use one cube or square to represent one person's data?

- **How do they represent the people who have lost zero teeth?**

- **Do they group and/or order their data?** If so, how?

- **Can you tell by looking at the representation what it is about?**

DIFFERENTIATION: Supporting the Range of Learners

Intervention Some students may have trouble finding a way to start this task. Ask students who are stuck to tell you verbally what they found out when they collected their data. Repeat what they say and then ask them how they could show what they just said. Make sure that it is clear that they need to include all the data that they collected in the representation.

Intervention If a few students are really stuck, suggest a way of representing the data that you think might make sense to them. Using self-stick notes might be good for some students because they can show each piece of data on a separate note and physically move the pieces around.

Intervention If a representation is unclear, ask one of the following questions to gain further insight into students' thinking and possibly help them clarify their ideas for displaying the data:

- **Can you tell me how you are showing your teeth data?**

- **How did you show the number of teeth lost by each student?**

- **Can you show me all the people who lost [4] teeth?**

ACTIVITY
② Describing Teeth Data

🕐 **20 MIN** 👥 **PAIRS**

When they have finished their representations, students will record two things they noticed about the number of teeth lost in the class they surveyed on *Student Activity Book* page 24.

When they are finished, they will switch representations with another pair and answer questions about that data on *Student Activity Book* page 25.

Students read and interpret data representations.

Name _____ Date _____

Pockets, Teeth, and Favorite Things

What Did You Find Out? ✏️

Look at your representation of the teeth data you collected from another class.

What do you notice about the number of teeth lost in this class?

Write two things you notice.

1. _____
   _____
   _____
   _____

2. _____
   _____
   _____
   _____

24 Unit 4   Session 2.5

▲ **Student Activity Book, p. 24**

Teaching Note

③ Save the Representations Students should save their representations of teeth data from another class for the next session.

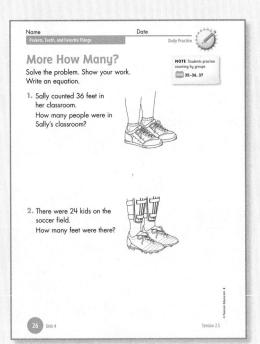

Name _____ Date _____

Pockets, Teeth, and Favorite Things

Explaining Someone Else's Findings

1. Who did you trade findings with?

   Names: _____ _____

   What class did they collect data from? _____

2. What was the most common number of teeth lost? _____

3. What was the fewest and most teeth lost in this class?

   Lowest _____ Highest _____

4. How many students lost fewer than 4 teeth? _____

5. How many students lost exactly 4 teeth? _____

6. How many students lost more than 4 teeth? _____

7. How many students were in this class? _____

8. What did you find surprising or unusual in this class's data?

   _____

   _____

   _____

Session 2.5   Unit 4 25

▲ Student Activity Book, p. 25

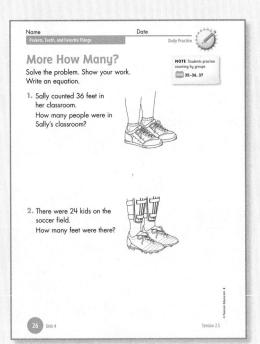

Name _____ Date _____

Pockets, Teeth, and Favorite Things   Daily Practice

More How Many?

Solve the problem. Show your work.
Write an equation.

NOTE Students practice counting by groups.
SMH 35–36, 37

1. Sally counted 36 feet in her classroom.
   How many people were in Sally's classroom?

2. There were 24 kids on the soccer field.
   How many feet were there?

26 Unit 4   Session 2.5

▲ Student Activity Book, p. 26

When you and your partner have finished answering the questions, meet with the team you switched representations with to see whether you have the answers they think you should have.

For example, if you said that the fewest number of teeth lost is 2, do they agree? Is that what they wanted to show? If they don't agree, there could be 2 reasons:

1. Maybe they didn't show their data as clearly as possible.

2. Maybe you didn't read the representation quite right.

If you disagree, work together to fix the problem.③

ONGOING ASSESSMENT: Observing Students at Work

Observe students as they write what they learned from the data they collected and then gather information from another representation.

- **Do students write reasonable conclusions about their data?**

- **Do the representations clearly communicate the findings, allowing students to answer all of the questions?**

- **Can students interpret a representation created by someone else to answer the questions about the data in the representation?**

SESSION FOLLOW-UP

③ Daily Practice

Daily Practice: For ongoing review, have students complete *Student Activity Book* page 26.

Student Math Handbook: Students and families may use *Student Math Handbook* pages 110, 111 for reference and review. See pages 145–147 in the back of the unit.

Comparing Teeth Data

Math Focus Points

◆ Comparing two sets of data

Today's Plan		Materials
① **ACTIVITY** **Comparing Teeth Data**	20 MIN PAIRS	• *Student Activity Book,* p. 27 • Teeth-data representations from other classes (from Session 2.5); teeth-data line plot*
② **DISCUSSION** **Comparing Teeth Data**	40 MIN PAIRS CLASS	• Teeth-data representations from other classes (from Session 2.5); self-stick note graph (from Session 2.3); chart paper
③ **SESSION FOLLOW-UP** **Daily Practice and Homework**		• *Student Activity Book,* pp. 28–29 • *Student Math Handbook,* pp. 110, 111

*See *Materials to Prepare,* p. 71.

Classroom Routines

Quick Images: Coins Using overhead coins, display 2 dimes and 5 pennies. Follow the basic *Quick Images* activity. Ask students to focus on the type and number of coins they saw as well as the value of the coins. When the coins are covered, ask students to explain how they determined how much money was displayed. Use equations to represent the problem and how students found the total. For example, $10¢ + 10¢ + 1¢ + 1¢ + 1¢ + 1¢ + 1¢ = 25¢$ or $10¢ + 10¢ + 5¢ = 25¢$. Repeat with 4 dimes and 2 pennies.

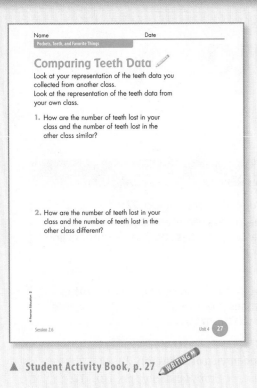

▲ Student Activity Book, p. 27 WRITING

Name _____ Date _____

Pockets, Teeth, and Favorite Things

Comparing Teeth Data ✏

Look at your representation of the teeth data you collected from another class.
Look at the representation of the teeth data from your own class.

1. How are the number of teeth lost in your class and the number of teeth lost in the other class similar?

2. How are the number of teeth lost in your class and the number of teeth lost in the other class different?

Session 2.6   Unit 4   27

ACTIVITY
① Comparing Teeth Data

20 MIN   PAIRS

Yesterday, you made a representation of the teeth data that you collected from another class and then you described what you noticed about the data. Today, you are going to compare the number of lost teeth in the class you visited with the number of lost teeth in our class.

First, you are going to work with your partner to compare the data. Then, the whole class will talk about how the number of lost teeth in other classrooms compares to the number of lost teeth in ours.

Hand out copies of the line plot you created of your students' teeth data from Session 2.3. Students will compare this representation with their own representations of teeth data from another class and then answer the questions on *Student Activity Book* page 27.

Students work together to compare teeth data from their class and another class.

ONGOING ASSESSMENT: Observing Students at Work ✔

Observe students as they compare the number of lost teeth in their own class with the number of lost teeth in another class.

- **Are students able to read and gather information from their own representation and from the line plot of their class's teeth data?**

- **Are students able to make accurate comparisons between the two data sets?**

- **What features of the data do students compare?** Do they compare the greatest and least values? Do they compare the number of people who lost a specific number of teeth? Do they compare the modes?

Professional Development

① **Dialogue Box:** Comparing Lost Teeth Data, p. 142

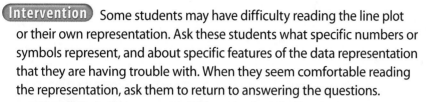

DIFFERENTIATION: Supporting the Range of Learners

Intervention Some students may have difficulty reading the line plot or their own representation. Ask these students what specific numbers or symbols represent, and about specific features of the data representation that they are having trouble with. When they seem comfortable reading the representation, ask them to return to answering the questions.

Intervention Some students may not be sure how to compare the data. Ask these students to describe one feature in one data set and then ask them to compare that specific feature with a similar feature in the other data set.

You said that many people in the first-grade class lost five teeth. How does that compare with our class? Did many people lose five teeth in our class? How many teeth did many people lose in our class?

DISCUSSION

2 Comparing Teeth Data

40 MIN   PAIRS   CLASS

Math Focus Points for Discussion

◆ Comparing two sets of data

During this discussion, students compare the teeth data they collected from other classrooms with the teeth data that they collected in their own classroom.① They will need their representations of the teeth data from other classes and they should sit next to their partner.

Post the self-stick note graph from Session 2.3 that shows your students' teeth data.

This was our representation of the teeth data that we collected from our own class. Look carefully at this graph and at the representation you made of the teeth data from another class. When we compare two sets of data, we want to make sure that we are looking at the same thing in each representation.

② Time Saver Consider having all of the students who visited the same grade level post their representations at the same time. Then the class can look at, for example, all of the fourth-grade data. Students would compare the data as a class and not separately by each pair. You would begin by comparing the data from the different fourth-grade classes and then comparing the fourth grade with your own class.

❸ Keep It Simple Because students have represented their data in different ways, some aspects of the data to compare may be less obvious. Keeping the comparisons simple will help. Although it might be interesting to try to compare all the different classes, it can be very overwhelming. Focus on comparing the teeth data from only your class with the teeth data of another class or grade, one at a time.

❹ Short on Time? If you do not have time to discuss all of the representations, you can return to them at other times during the day and over the next few days.

Compare what we found out from our class with what you found out from another class.

• How is the number of teeth lost by students in our class similar to the number of teeth lost in the other class?

• How are the numbers different?

• Is there anything surprising?

Talk with your partner about what you notice. In a few minutes, you are going to share what you noticed with the class.

Choose one pair of students to share their representation.❷ Hang the representation next to the representation of your class's teeth data. Ask the pair to share one or two things they noticed when they compared the data from the two classes. If students are not sure what to look for, here are some easy comparisons to make:❸

• The greatest and fewest number of lost teeth in each class;

• The same data points ("Two people in our class lost four teeth and six people in the other class lost four teeth.");

• The most common number of teeth lost by students in each class;

• Any surprising or unusual pieces of data.

Students share their findings and compare another class's data to their own.

Allow the rest of the class a little time to share anything that they noticed in comparing the two classes. As students share their observations, record them on chart paper to hang up with their representations.❹

If you have time, return to the predictions students made in Session 2.4 about the number of teeth they thought might be lost in other classrooms. Ask students whether they can tell from the representations whether their predictions were correct.

SESSION FOLLOW-UP
Daily Practice and Homework

 Daily Practice: For ongoing review, have students complete *Student Activity Book* page 28.

 Homework: On *Student Activity Book* page 29, students play *Guess My Rule* with two rules.

 Student Math Handbook: Students and families may use *Student Math Handbook* pages 110, 111 for reference and review. See pages 145–147 in the back of this unit.

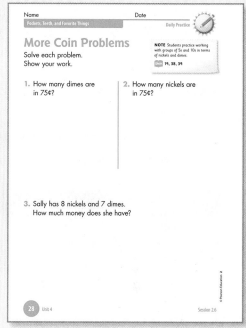

▲ **Student Activity Book, p. 28**

▲ **Student Activity Book, p. 29**

Mystery Teeth Data

Math Focus Points

- Representing data on a line plot
- Describing important features of a data set
- Developing a hypothesis based on a set of data

Today's Plan		Materials
ACTIVITY ❶ **Mystery Teeth Data**	30 MIN GROUPS INDIVIDUALS	• M53–M56* • Teeth-data representation from other classes (from Session 2.5)
ACTIVITY ❷ **Which Class Is It?**	10 MIN INDIVIDUALS	• *Student Activity Book*, pp. 31–32 • Chart paper*
DISCUSSION ❸ **Which Class Is It?**	20 MIN CLASS	• Charts: "Class A," "Class B," "Class C," "Class D"
SESSION FOLLOW-UP ❹ **Daily Practice**		• *Student Activity Book*, p. 33 • *Student Math Handbook*, pp. 110, 111

*See *Materials to Prepare*, p. 71.

Classroom Routines

Today's Number: 44 Using Dimes and Pennies   Students individually generate numerical expressions for the number 44, using all possible combinations of dimes and pennies. Students then list at least 5 other expressions for 44 using addition and/or subtraction. They record these expressions on blank paper, which they have labeled with the date and heading "Today's Number: 44". This work will give you some information on how students are understanding and working with *Today's Number*. This is the fourth in a series of *Today's Number* work samples that will be collected throughout the year.

ACTIVITY

Mystery Teeth Data

30 MIN   GROUPS   INDIVIDUALS

Students make line plots of sets of Mystery Teeth Data. Introduce this activity by making a line plot, using one of the sets of data that students collected from another classroom.

Today we are going to do an activity with some Mystery Teeth Data from other classrooms. To do this activity, you need to make a line plot of a set of teeth data. Do you remember when we made a line plot of our pocket data? To help you remember how to make a line plot, I am going to make one using the set of data that [Carla and Henry] collected from the [third grade].

Ask a student to look at the data and identify the fewest number of lost teeth in this particular class and the greatest number of lost teeth. Then make a line plot, using this range of numbers.

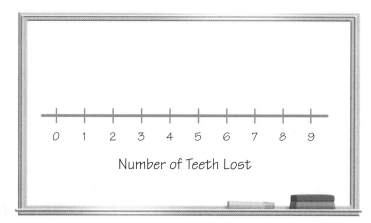

[Henry] told me that the fewest number of lost teeth was zero and the greatest number was nine. I am going to make my line plot start at zero and end at nine. The data in this set range from zero to nine.

Ask a student to read aloud each name and the number of teeth that each student lost. Record the data on the line plot. Briefly discuss the representation by pointing to one of the Xs.

What does this X mean? What do four Xs on 3 mean?

Teaching Note

❶ **If Students Finish Early** If some students finish early, they can choose another set of data to represent.

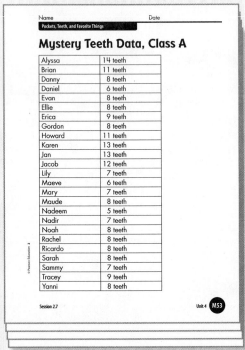

Name _____ Date _____

Pockets, Teeth, and Favorite Things

Mystery Teeth Data, Class A

Alyssa	14 teeth
Brian	11 teeth
Danny	8 teeth
Daniel	6 teeth
Evan	8 teeth
Ellie	8 teeth
Erica	9 teeth
Gordon	8 teeth
Howard	11 teeth
Karen	13 teeth
Jan	13 teeth
Jacob	12 teeth
Lily	7 teeth
Maeve	6 teeth
Mary	7 teeth
Maude	8 teeth
Nadeem	5 teeth
Nadir	7 teeth
Noah	8 teeth
Rachel	8 teeth
Ricardo	8 teeth
Sarah	8 teeth
Sammy	7 teeth
Tracey	9 teeth
Yanni	8 teeth

Session 2.7   Unit 4 M53

▲ Resource Masters, M53–M56

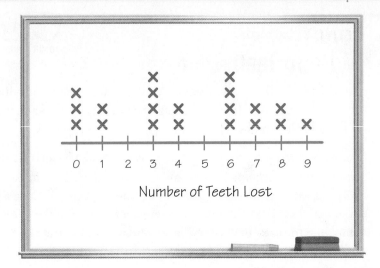

Number of Teeth Lost

Discuss any questions students have about making a line plot. Remind students to figure out the greatest and fewest number of lost teeth before they make their line plot.

Distribute 1 of the 4 Mystery Teeth Data sheets (M53–M56) to each student. Try to distribute the 4 pages as evenly as possible across the class.

Keep the grade levels secret for now. (You will find the grade levels for the Mystery Teeth Data on page 107.)

These data have been collected from 4 different classes at other schools. Each of you will make a representation on paper of the data that you get.

Hand out a blank sheet of paper to each student.

You each have one set of Mystery Teeth Data to work with. The first thing you are going to do is make a line plot of the data on paper.

Have students write their names on their work and label the line plot "Number of Teeth Lost," but remind them not to write the letter of the class they are representing. You may want to have students record their letter on a scrap of paper and put it in their math folder.❶

ONGOING ASSESSMENT: Observing Students at Work

Observe students as they make line plots of a set of mystery data.

- **Do students determine the greatest and least values before starting their line plot?** Do students write all of the numbers from the least value to the greatest value on their line plot or only those numbers with data?

- **Do students understand what the numbers stand for and what the Xs stand for?**

- **Do students account for all of the pieces of data on their line plots (e.g., 24 responses, 24 pieces of data)?**

DIFFERENTIATION: Supporting the Range of Learners

Intervention Some students may have difficulty creating a line plot of the Mystery Teeth Data, even if they created their own representations of numerical data in past sessions. To help, begin by asking them the greatest and fewest number of lost teeth in their mystery data. Have them write these numbers under a line and fill in the numbers in between. Help them systematically go down the list and place each data point on the line.

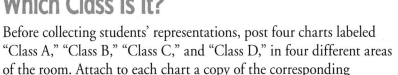

ACTIVITY
2 Which Class Is It?

10 MIN INDIVIDUALS

Before collecting students' representations, post four charts labeled "Class A," "Class B," "Class C," and "Class D," in four different areas of the room. Attach to each chart a copy of the corresponding Mystery Teeth Data sheet (M53–M56). Students will post their representations on the charts.

Collect students' mystery data representations, mix them up, and redistribute them so that each student has a representation other than his or her own.

Students will now be working on *Student Activity Book* pages 31–32.

Look at the representation you have just received and see whether you can match it to one of the sets of Mystery Teeth Data on *Student Activity Book* page 31. When you think you know which data set your line plot represents, put your representation on the right chart, and then answer the questions in your *Student Activity Book* on page 32. ❷

Teaching Note

❷ **Note Inaccuracies** If students find inaccuracies on the representation, suggest that they note this on *Student Activity Book* page 32.

▲ Student Activity Book, p. 31

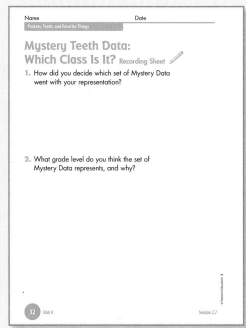

▲ Student Activity Book, p. 32

Students post Mystery Teeth Data line plots.

ONGOING ASSESSMENT: Observing Students at Work

Students match a set of unordered data to a line plot representation.

- **What aspects of the graph did students pay particular attention to as they made their decision?** The greatest and least values? The modes? The number of data points at each value?

- **Do students mostly use the overall shape of the data to match the data sets, or do they mostly look at specific data points?** Do they look at multiple aspects of the data or focus on certain aspects?

- **Do students correctly match the line plot to the data set?**

- **Do students use some of the data that they collected from other classrooms to determine what grade the Mystery Teeth Data might be from?**

DIFFERENTIATION: Supporting the Range of Learners

Intervention If students have difficulty reading a line plot and gathering information from it, ask them about what specific Xs mean and what the numbers stand for.

Intervention Some students may have difficulty looking for clues in the line plot to help them figure out which mystery data it matches. To help them get started, ask the following questions:

What do you notice about the line plot you have? See whether any of the mystery data have that aspect.

If students have trouble describing aspects of the line plot, ask them to look for specific aspects, such as these:

- The greatest and least number of lost teeth
- The number of teeth that most students have lost
- A number of teeth that no one has lost

DISCUSSION
Which Class Is It?

20 MIN   CLASS

Math Focus Points for Discussion
◆ Developing a hypothesis based on a set of data

Let's look at the representations that you posted for Class A.❸ ❺ If you think the line plot you posted represented the data from this class, can you explain why? Were there certain things about the graph that made you think it belonged to this set of data?❹

Depending on how the discussion goes, you may want to have students make some hypotheses about what grade each class represents as they discuss each set of data. They will make these hypotheses on the basis of the data and the representations. You also might discuss all the sets of Mystery Teeth Data and then end the discussion with students offering their ideas and hypotheses about which data represent which grade level.

If you complete the discussion during this session, you will want to reveal the grade level that each data set represents. By this time, each student's representation should be matched correctly.

SESSION FOLLOW-UP
Daily Practice

 Daily Practice: For reinforcement of this unit's content, have students complete *Student Activity Book* page 33.

Student Math Handbook: Students and families may use *Student Math Handbook* pages 110, 111 for reference and review. See pages 145–147 in the back of this unit.

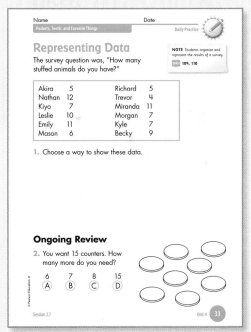

▲ Student Activity Book, p. 33

End-of-Unit Assessment

Math Focus Points

◆ Ordering, representing, and describing a set of numerical data

◆ Describing what the data show about the group surveyed

◆ Interpreting a data representation including a line plot

◆ Comparing two sets of data

◆ Sorting a set of data by two attributes at one time

◆ Using a Venn diagram to represent a sorted set of data

Today's Plan		Materials
① ACTIVITY **How Many Books in a Week?**	10 MIN CLASS	• Class list
② ASSESSMENT ACTIVITY **End-of-Unit Assessment**	50 MIN INDIVIDUALS	• M57–M59* • Class list (1 per student)*
③ SESSION FOLLOW-UP **Daily Practice**		• *Student Activity Book*, p. 34 • *Student Math Handbook*, pp. 108, 110, 111

*See *Materials to Prepare*, p. 71.

Classroom Routines

What Time Is It? What Time Will It Be? Ask students to display 2:00 on their small clocks as you write 2:00 on the board.

In 2 hours what time will it be?

Students set the new time on their clocks and talk with their partner about what time it will be and how they know. Then ask them how that time would look on a digital clock (4:00). Do several of these, varying the start time (whole and half hours), and the time elapsed between 2 and 4 hours. Each time discuss what the time would look like on a digital clock and how many times the minute hand traveled around the clock.

ACTIVITY
How Many Books in a Week?

10 MIN · CLASS

To do the End-of-Unit Assessment problems, students will need data on how many books students in the class read in a week. If it is the middle of the week, you will need to decide whether to use the last week ending on Sunday or to go from the middle of the week to the middle of the next week. Give each student a class list.

Think about how many books you have read in the last week. If you're not sure exactly how many you have read, you can estimate about *how many.*

Go through the class list and ask each student how many books he or she has read. Have each student record the numbers on his or her own class list.

ASSESSMENT ACTIVITY
End-of-Unit Assessment

50 MIN · INDIVIDUALS

There are three End-of-Unit Assessment tasks. In the first task, students represent a set of numerical data and describe the data (Benchmarks 3 and 4). In the second task, students read and interpret a line plot and compare two sets of data (Benchmarks 5 and 6). In the final task, students sort data by two rules, using a Venn diagram (Benchmark 1).

Begin by reading through the first two problems together. Students should work on these two problems first.

In Problem 1 (M57), students represent and describe the data about the number of books students in their class read in a week. In Problem 2 (M58), students look at a line plot of similar data collected from a third-grade classroom and describe various aspects of the data. They will then compare their book data from their second-grade class with the third-grade data.

As small groups of students finish the first two problems, read through Problem 3 (M59) with them. In this problem, students sort a set of names according to two rules as they did in *Guess My Rule* with Two Rules.

As students finish the end of the assessment, ask students whom you have not assessed on the Plus Ten combinations to meet with you. (Benchmark 7)

Professional Development

Teacher Note: End-of-Unit Assessment, p. 126

▲ Resource Master, M57

▲ Resource Masters, M58–M59

Differentiation

❷ English Language Learners Sorting the names may be challenging for some English Language Learners due to the amount of print involved. You may need to read the list of names aloud to them before they begin the task. English Language Learners may also have trouble writing their rules in English; if so, let students explain their rules verbally and then help them put their ideas into writing.

Name _____ Date _____

Pockets, Teeth, and Favorite Things   Daily Practice

Organizing Data

Jen's favorite animal is a dog. She loves big dogs and little dogs. She loves dogs with long hair or short hair. She loves dogs that are brown, black or white.

NOTE Students solve real-world problems involving the math content of this unit.
SMH 106–107

One day at the park, Jen counted 8 dogs. Here are the dogs she saw.

How can Jen sort the dogs?
Think of two rules. Write the rules below.

First way	Second way

34   Unit 4   Session 2.8

▲ **Student Activity Book, p. 34**

✓ **ONGOING ASSESSMENT: Observing Students at Work**

Observe students as they complete the three assessment problems.

Problem 1: How Many Books in a Week?

- **Are students able to organize and represent their data in a clear way?** Do students represent all the data? Do they represent the data accurately?

- **Are students' descriptive statements about the data accurate?** Are students able to connect the data to what it tells them about the class?

Problem 2: Third Graders: How Many Books in a Week?

- **Are students able to use the line plot to determine how many students read a given number of books in a week?**

- **Are students able to draw conclusions about the third-grade class from the line plot?**

- **Are students able to make comparisons between the two classes?**

Problem 3: Guess My Rule with Names❷

- **Do students choose rules that fit the attributes of the names?**

- **Are they able to place the names in the appropriate places, including those that fit both of the rules?**

SESSION FOLLOW-UP

③ Daily Practice

Daily Practice: For enrichment, have students complete *Student Activity Book* page 34.

Student Math Handbook: Students and families may use *Student Math Handbook* pages 108, 110, 111 for reference and review. See pages 145–147 in the back of this unit.

Pockets, Teeth, and Favorite Things

Teacher Notes

In Part 6 of *Implementing Investigations in Grade 2,* you will find a set of Teacher Notes that addresses topics and issues applicable to the curriculum as a whole rather than to specific curriculum units. They include the following:

Computational Fluency and Place Value

Computational Algorithms and Methods

Representations and Contexts for Mathematical Work

Foundations of Algebra in the Elementary Grades

Discussing Mathematical Ideas

Racial and Linguistic Diversity in the Classroom:
  What Does Equity Mean in Today's Math Classroom?

Dialogue Boxes

Assessment: Assessing the Plus Ten Combinations

During this unit, you will need to find time to assess students on the +10 combinations, which were introduced in Unit 3, *Stickers, Number Strings, and Story Problems*. When students are working independently on an activity, work with individuals or small groups to assess their fluency with these combinations.

Use a set of +10 Combinations Cards from Unit 3, *Stickers, Number Strings, and Story Problems*. Read aloud each card as the student looks at it, and then ask for the answer. Record your observations on the Assessment Checklist: +10 Combinations (M51). Throughout this unit there will be reminders to do this assessment, but you will need to choose the times that work best for you.

By the end of this unit, students are expected to be fluent with the +10 combinations (Benchmark 7). Students are likely to fall into these 3 groups:

Fluent These students know all or almost all of the +10 combinations. They can hear or read a problem, think for a moment, and then say the answer. Most second graders should be in this category at this point in the year.

Nearly Fluent These students are fluent with many of the +10 combinations, but they pause to figure out the answer to some. Note the combinations with which students are not yet fluent, and check that these match the cards in their "Combinations I'm Still Working On" envelopes, which they made in Unit 1, *Counting, Coins, and Combinations*. Also, point out troublesome combinations to students. For example, you might say, "You've come a long way with these combinations, but a few still seem to be giving you some trouble. How could we make it easier for you to remember that $10 + 9$ and $9 + 10$ equal 19?" You might assign students two combinations per week to work on until they know them all.

Not Yet Fluent These students use their fingers to count up, or use cubes to model, many of the +10 combinations. There should be very few students in this category.

Students who are nearly fluent and not yet fluent need more practice with +10 combinations and should use their addition cards to practice. Work with students to write clues for the cards. Students will also benefit from using concrete models to examine what happens when 10 is added to a number. Give them the opportunity to solve +10 problems by using the 100 chart, a number line, and cubes (with some cubes stacked in towers of 10).

When Students Represent Data

When students create their own ways of representing data, they often come up with pictures or graphs that powerfully communicate the meaning of the data. Students may be familiar with many commonly used representations such as bar graphs and tallies, but they should be encouraged to develop their own pictures and graphs as well.

In the ongoing history of visual representation of data, many unusual forms of graphs and diagrams have been developed. Some of the most striking graphs were devised by statisticians or scientists to represent a single, unusual data set in a new way. Even now, new standard forms are taking their place in the statistician's repertoire beside the more familiar bar graph or histogram.

Therefore, although we do want students to use and interpret standard forms of graphs, we also want them to learn that, like other mathematicians and scientists, they can represent data in their own individual ways. Their pictures, diagrams, and graphs are important tools in the data analysis process.

Through constructing their own representations, students can become more familiar with the data, understand the data better, and begin to develop theories about the data. Also, if they are going to "publish" their findings, they can communicate what they know about the data to an audience.

Students can make graphs and representations with pencil and paper, connecting cubes, or stick-on notes. Cubes and stick-on notes offer flexibility because they can be easily rearranged. Encourage students to construct concrete and pictorial representations of their data by using connecting cubes, pictures, or even the actual objects.

Encourage students to try different forms of representation until they discover one that works well in organizing their data. Students in the second grade are capable of making simple but effective sketches and pictures of the data they collect. Katrina and Leo represented their *Guess My Rule* data as shown. They do not follow a standard graph or table form but show the data clearly and effectively.

Katrina's Work

Leo's Work

Teacher Note

Attribute Materials: About the Yektti Cards

Yekttis (YEK-tees) are fantasy creatures from outer space. They have between 1 and 4 antennae, 2 types of eyes (ringed or plain), and 4 head shapes (square, triangle, rhombus, or hexagon). The Yektti Cards are a set of attribute cards—cards that one can sort and classify according to the characteristics of the set. Like other attribute materials, this set is structured so that there is 1 Yektti with each possible combination of characteristics. For example, there is 1 triangular Yektti with 3 antennae and ringed eyes, 1 triangular Yektti with 3 antennae and plain eyes, 1 square Yektti with 3 antennae and plain eyes, and so on.

Unlike most sets of related things in the real world, the Yektti set has only 3 attributes (number of antennae, head shape, and eye type). Students have already dealt with a more complex set that has endless possibilities for classification—themselves—and later in this unit they will develop their own categories for groups of things with much less well-defined characteristics. Attribute materials like the Yekttis are useful precisely because of their limited characteristics.

Because the Yekttis can be sorted into only a few easily deduced categories, students can concentrate on making careful observations and reasoning from evidence. In this investigation, students engage in sorting activities that require them to take into account more than 1 attribute at a time. The Yekttis help students learn about more complex sorting in a context that is not too overwhelming.

The Yektti Materials

A complete set of Yektti Cards contains 32 individual Yekttis, 1 with each possible combination of head shape, eye type, and number of antennae. For this investigation, you will need 1 set of Large Yektti Cards for whole-class work and a set of Small Yektti Cards for each group.

Attribute materials are sets of blocks or drawings on cards that vary in shape, color, size, or other characteristics. The Yekttis in this unit are one such set. Working with other types of sorting materials, such as attribute block sets, logic blocks, or related materials, is an appropriate extension throughout this unit. The game *Guess My Rule,* as well as many other activities in which students investigate classification, can be done with these materials.

Sorting, Classifying, and Categorical Data

Sorting and classifying are central scientific, mathematical, and human activities. Important issues of classification arise in many disciplines. For example:

- How can we classify the books in a library in a systematic and useful way?

- Is this animal a new species or is it part of a class of animals that has already been identified and described?

As children learn about their world, community, language, and culture, they develop and organize categories of information, asking such questions as these:

- Which foods are fruits?

- Which animals are dogs?

- Which behaviors are accepted at my house, at Grandma's house, or in the park?

- To which words can you add *-ed* to form the past tense?

In the broadest sense, classification is about how things (people, animals, numbers, shapes, attitudes) are alike or different. Sorting any collection into categories requires attending to certain attributes and ignoring others. It is this skill of focusing on particular attributes and excluding others that primary-grade students learn. For example, in order to identify a shape as a triangle, we attend only to these certain characteristics:

- The number of sides and angles

- The fact that each side is a line segment

- Whether the shape is closed (without breaks or gaps)

We do not pay attention to size, color, texture, or orientation of the shape in order to identify it as a triangle. Knowing what to focus on and what to ignore may be an innate skill for adults, but the concept of classifying by particular attributes is an important area of learning for young students. This unit begins with activities in which students sort by visible attributes—people who are or are not wearing a watch; Yekttis with 1, 2, 3, or 4 antenna; and

so on. Students learn to pay attention to certain attributes and to ways in which things go together.

What Is Categorical Data?

In this unit, students encounter two kinds of data. We refer to these as *categorical data* and *numerical data*. Investigation 1 focuses on categorical data—data that have values that can be classified in categories but cannot be ordered by numerical value. For example, consider the question "What color eyes do you have?" Possible data values for this question include blue, brown, hazel, and gray. A bar graph could be made showing the frequencies with which each of these data values occurs.

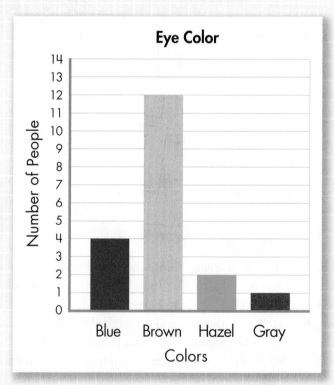

The values of the data can be classified and graphed, but they do not have an inherent order; hazel is not *more* or *less* than brown or blue.

The numerical data that students collect and analyze in Investigation 2 consist of numerical values that can be ordered and compared mathematically, such as the number of pockets students are wearing or the number of teeth they have lost. See **Teacher Note:** Describing Numerical Data, page 122.

Second graders often describe their data by listing the count of each categorical value. In particular, students are likely to notice a value that has more data than any other category. This value is the *mode* of the data set. For example, if 10 students like sweets, 6 like fruit, and 8 like pizza, the mode is sweets. However, notice that the *mode* may not always be synonymous with *most*. In the eye color graph, most of the people do have brown eyes, but in the favorite food example, 14 students chose either fruit or pizza, and only 10 chose sweets.

Classifying Categorical Data

In Investigation 1, students collect data about favorite weekend activities and then organize the data into categories. As they classify the data in different ways, students impose order. By doing so, they can ask different questions about the data set, such as these:

• Do students prefer outdoor or indoor activities?

• Do students prefer reading, board games, or sports?

Students learn how the questions they can address depend on how the data are organized.

Some categorical data, such as the eye-color data, can be easily classified into a few categories. But a more varied set of categorical data, such as favorite-weekend-activities data, can be more difficult to organize. If the data are grouped according to individual activities, one might end up with a graph like this one, which has many categories with only 1 or 2 pieces of data in each.

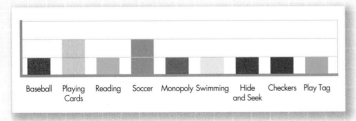

It is difficult to make any comparisons or draw any conclusions when the data are organized in this way. However, when the data are grouped in the following way, some interesting comparisons can emerge:

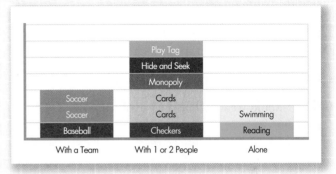

Be mindful of the fact that students will often choose nonparallel categories or categories that do not seem to go together. For example, this student divides responses to "What is your favorite food?" into cheese foods, noodle foods, sea foods, meat foods, and white foods.

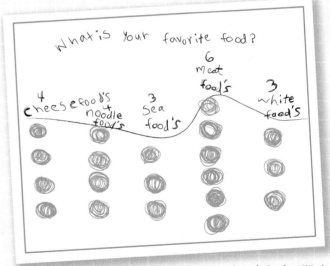

Sample Student Work

This classification is quite an interesting one. The student is thinking hard about how important ingredients of the foods can be used to classify them. However, the "white foods" category does not fit with the other categories and may have been a way of putting together responses that did not fit anywhere else. Expect this use of nonparallel categories from second graders. However, ask students to think about why they chose a particular category. ("I noticed that all your other categories are about what's in the food, and this one is about color. Why did you switch to color?")

Throughout their work, students will encounter key problems in data organization, such as the following:

- What makes a good category?

- What should we do when a piece of data does not fit in any category?

These issues stem from real dilemmas about data analysis and are related to the following questions:

- What is it we are trying to find out?

- Will our choice help us see our information more clearly or will it obscure important information?

A key role for the teacher is to help students connect the decisions they make to *what they can find out* from their data.

Assessment: What's Your Favorite Food?

There are two parts to Assessment: What's Your Favorite Food? (M47–M48). In the first part, students sort a data set into categories and make a representation. In the second part, students interpret the data.

Problem 1: Sorting Data into Categories

Benchmark addressed:

Benchmark 2: Identify categories for a set of categorical data and organize the data into chosen categories.

In order to meet the benchmark, students' work should show that they can:

- Group data into categories on the basis of similar attributes;

- Represent the data sorted into categories so that the categories and the data are clear and distinct.

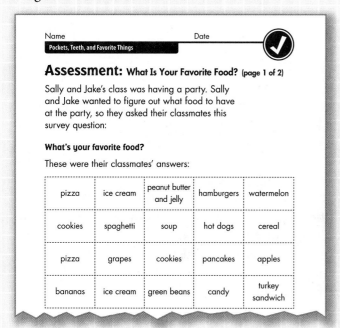

▲ Resource Masters, M47

Meeting the Benchmark

The following student work samples provide a range of typical responses. All of these students meet the benchmark because:

- They organize the data into clear categories and label them;

- They represent the data set accurately;

- They use various categories to sort the data.

Some students will create a set of categories that are consistent in theme or subject matter. They may sort the data into categories such as these:

- Hot foods and cold foods

- Hard foods and soft foods

- Crunchy foods and smooth foods

- Foods you eat with a fork, a spoon, or your hands

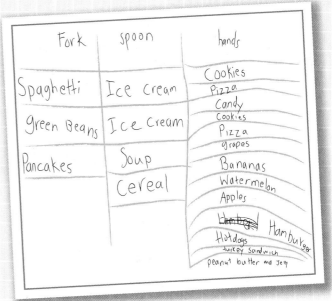

Rochelle's Work

Some students may sort the data according to generally accepted nutritional food groups.

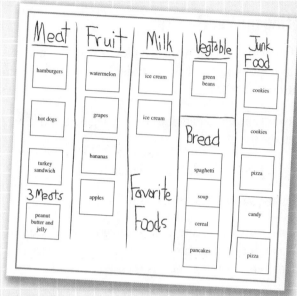

Travis's Work

Some students may sort the data into categories that are clear but not consistent in theme or subject matter. For example, Chen's groups covered a variety of subject areas, including food groups, whether the food is healthful, and at what meal the food is eaten.

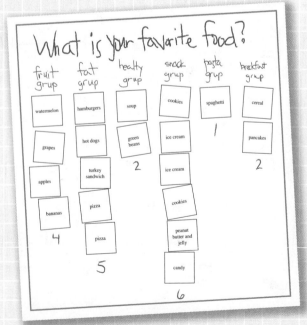

Chen's Work

Although it will eventually be a goal for students to sort data into categories that are consistent in subject matter, it is not a benchmark for this unit.

Partially Meeting the Benchmark

Some students may create clear, distinct categories but may not give them names that correctly describe the category.

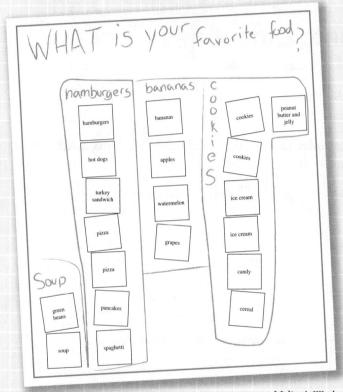

Melissa's Work

Choosing ways to describe the categories is an important element of organizing and representing data. Students who have difficulty verbalizing or writing ideas may have difficulty naming categories and may need some support. Others may see some similarities in the data they grouped together but may not realize that there could be a general name for the category. To help these students, ask questions such as the following:

• Why did you group these foods together?

• What is the same about them?

• What could you call this group of foods?

Some students may come up with 1 or 2 categories to sort similar data but then leave the rest of the data in its own group. These students should be encouraged to look for ways that all of the data can be put into categories similar to those that they have already created.

Not Meeting the Benchmark

Students who do not meet the benchmark may still be constructing what it means to organize data into categories.

Many students who do not meet the benchmark will, like Nadia, put only pieces of data that are identical together in categories.

Nadia's Work

A few students will put each piece of data in a separate category. These students may not understand what it means to put data into categories on the basis of similar attributes and may not understand how grouping the data into categories will help them gain more information about the results of a survey. These students will benefit from more opportunities to sort data into categories. Playing *Guess My Rule* with data such as foods, animals, and names will give them an opportunity to examine how data are similar and how they can be grouped together.

Having opportunities to sort survey results will help students connect to the purpose of sorting data. Guide students in their sorting by asking questions such as the following:

- What do you notice about the favorite foods of students in this class?

- How could we sort these data to learn more about the favorite foods of students in this class?

- How are some of students' favorite foods similar?

You may also choose to point out how you would sort the data. For example, say, "I noticed that many people like fruit. Let's put those foods together."

Students who do not meet the benchmark may not yet understand the purpose of making a representation or how to organize a set of data and make a representation that communicates information to others. All students will have more opportunities in this unit to represent sets of data. As the students who did not meet the benchmark in this assessment create other representations in subsequent sessions, help them focus on a representation as a means of communicating information by asking questions such as the following:

- How can you show someone who is not in this class what we found out?

- What will someone who is not in this class be able to find out from your representation?

- How can you make a representation so that it is easy to see that (12 people lost 5 teeth and 10 people lost 4)?

Problem 2: Interpreting the Data

Benchmark addressed:

Benchmark 5: Read and interpret a variety of representations of numerical and categorical data.

In order to meet this benchmark, students must be able to state what they learned about the group surveyed, given the way they categorized the data.

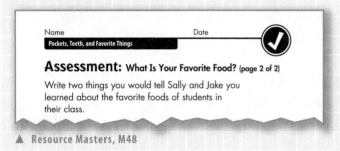

Name _____ Date _____ ✓

Pockets, Teeth, and Favorite Things

Assessment: What Is Your Favorite Food? (page 2 of 2)

Write two things you would tell Sally and Jake you learned about the favorite foods of students in their class.

▲ **Resource Masters, M48**

Meeting the Benchmark

The following student work samples provide a range of typical responses. All of these students meet the benchmark because:

• They interpret the data by making two statements about what they learned about the group, given their categorization of the data;

• Their work varies in what they claim to have learned from the data.

Many students will compare the amount of data in the categories, stating which categories have more data than others and which have less. For example, students may state which types of foods more or less students chose as their favorites. Some students may not yet make the distinction between "most" and "more." For example, they may state that *most* students' favorite foods were breads when, in fact, *more* students' favorite foods were breads.

On my gragh I noticed most peole voted forlunch foods.less people voted for icecream and things that are made the bread group.

Katrina's Work

I found out that More people likemeat food. I found out that less people like fruit fruit food.

Amaya's Work

Some students may also state the quantity of data in certain categories, such as how many students chose a certain type of food as their favorite.

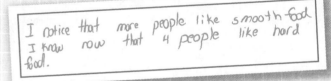

I notice that more people like smooth food I know now that 4 people like hard food.

Leo's Work

A few students may further quantify their comparisons by stating how many more students chose certain types of foods. For example, students may observe that more people chose hot foods than cold foods, but only a few more.

Partially Meeting the Benchmark

Some students may write statements that compare the quantities in the categories but do not explain what the information reveals about the people surveyed. For example, Gregory wrote, "The meat column has more than the others. The least amount of food is vegetables."

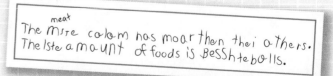

The meat mare colom has moar then thei others. The lste amount of foods is BeSShtebolls.

Gregory's Work

From these statements, it is unclear whether Gregory understands the connection between the amount of data in each category and what it tells about the people surveyed. Gregory's teacher might say to him, "The smallest group is vegetables and the biggest group is meat. What does that tell you about the favorite foods of students in the class?" In order to meet the benchmark, Gregory might respond, "Less people like vegetables and more people like meat."

Some students may correctly describe the data in their statements, but they may not use the categories they created in their descriptions of the data. For example, Alberto wrote about the number of people who liked pizza and ice cream, even though the categories he used were milk, bread, and fruit.

> I note ist that two pepole like pizza and two other philcrin like ice cream.

Alberto's Work

Ask these students to describe what they learned, according to the categories they came up with and the way in which they sorted the data. For some students, this encouragement may be enough for them to make statements based on their categories. Others may still be looking at only single pieces of data and not yet connecting what their categories tell them about the group surveyed. Ask these students specifically about their categories and what they show about the favorite foods of students in this class. For example, say, "You sorted students' favorite foods into hot foods and cold foods. What can you say about whether students prefer hot or cold foods?"

Students who put together only identical pieces of data in the first part of the assessment may make correct statements about the data in the second part. However, because they did not put the data into categories, their statements do not meet the benchmark. These students need more experience sorting data.

> a lot of people like pizza and cookies in arthur and Desiree class!

Nadia's Work

Some students may make only one statement about the data. Encourage these students to make another.

Not Meeting the Benchmark

Students who do not meet the benchmark may still be constructing what it means to describe and interpret a set of data. They may make statements about the data that neither compare the quantities in the categories nor relate the data to what it tells about the group surveyed.

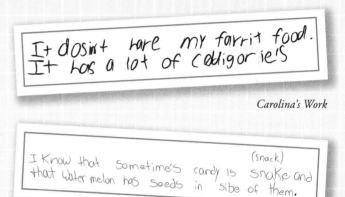

> It dosint hare my farrit food. It has a lot of cadigorie's

Carolina's Work

> I know that sometime's candy is snake and (snack) that water melon has seeds in sibe of them.

Holly's Work

Alternatively, these students may come to incorrect conclusions that do not match their categorization of the data.

These students may not yet understand how to gather information from a representation of a sorted set of data. Moreover, they may not know what information is important to look for. These students will benefit from more opportunities to read representations of data and describe the information they can gather from them. To help students describe representations, ask questions such as the following:

- What can we find out from this representation about the favorite foods of students in this class?

- Are there any kinds of foods that more students said were their favorites?

- How many students' favorite foods were sweets?

Teacher Note

Describing Numerical Data

In Unit 4, Investigation 2, students work with numerical data. In statistics, there are different kinds of numerical, or quantitative, data that behave in different ways. In this unit, students work with data that result from counting something—the number of pockets students are wearing, the number of teeth students have lost, and so on. These data can be ordered by value and along a scale, as in the following line plot.

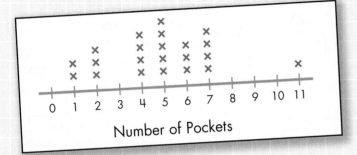

Number of Pockets

A line plot is one quick way to organize numerical data. Line plots work especially well for numerical data with a small range.

By looking at the data in order, we can see the *range* of the data. We can also see the shape of the data and how they are distributed across the range—where they are concentrated, where they are spread out, where there are gaps in the data, and whether there is an *outlier*.

Most second graders describe numerical data in ways similar to the ways they describe categorical data. They report the number of pieces of data at each value: 2 people had 1 pocket, 3 people had 2 pockets, and so on. Students are also likely to notice the *mode,* a value that has more data than any other value. For example, students may notice that more people had 5 pockets than any other number of pockets.

In Grade 3, an emphasis is placed on the shift from seeing each value as separate to describing the data set as a whole. However, second graders can begin to move beyond simply listing the amount of data at each value and noticing where data are concentrated. Comparing two or more groups

motivates students to look at the overall shape of the data. See **Dialogue Box:** Comparing Lost Teeth Data (page 142) for an example.

This system of describing data cannot be done with categorical data. Categorical data are not quantities, so we cannot put them in order. They do not have a range or outliers. It is not possible to talk about where categorical data are clumped or concentrated because there is no inherent order to the categories. A "clump" may result from an accidental juxtaposition of categories, but the clump would disappear if these categories were ordered differently on a graph. In contrast, it makes sense to describe the concentration of data in the line plot above; most students in the class have between 4 and 7 pockets.

As students describe numerical data, introduce the following statistical terms.

Mode The mode is the value that has appeared the most frequently in the data set. The mode of the data set shown above is 5 pockets. There can be more than one mode in a set of data. For example, if there were also 5 people who had 7 pockets, there would be 2 modes.

The mode is easy for second graders to identify. However, the mode does not always indicate something important about the set of data. In the data set above, the mode has about a quarter of the data. In addition, the mode is part of a larger clump of data. This mode is an important indicator of what is going on in this data set. However, look at the mode in the data set shown below.

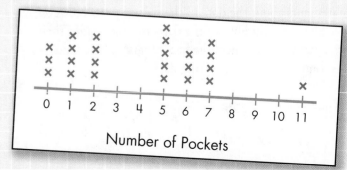

Number of Pockets

In this data set, the mode is also 5 pockets. However, the mode is not such a significant feature of these data. When you look at the overall shape of the data, you notice that there are two clumps of data—from 0 to 2 pockets and from 5 to 7 pockets. Each clump has close to half the data. The mode alone does not tell enough about the overall story of this data set. The two clumps of data are more indicative of the situation represented.

Range The range of the data is technically the difference between the highest and lowest values in the data set. In the first line plot shown, the range of the data is 10, the difference between 1 and 11. It is important for second graders to notice the minimum and maximum values. Students often talk about the minimum and maximum values by saying, "The data range from 1 to 11," or "The range is from 1 to 11."

Outlier An outlier is a value that is much higher or much lower than other values in the data set. Statisticians have developed formulas for determining how much higher or lower a value must be in order to define it as an outlier. In this unit, students work with the idea of an outlier without having a particular mathematical rule. They look for values that are unusual and think about what might account for that value. In the two line plots of pocket data, the outlier is 11 pockets.

Students' Representations of Numerical Data

In second grade, students are still learning about how to use representations that show the frequency of the occurrence of each value in their data. In first grade, they were introduced to bar graphs. In this unit, they will focus on line plots. Just as students learned to group their categorical data, here they learn to group their numerical data. For numerical data, these groups are determined by the values of the data.

There are two basic types of representations that you are likely to see in your class. One type shows each individual's data as a quantity by using a tower of cubes, a bar on a graph, or a column of **Xs.** For example, Henry represented the number of lost teeth in the graph below:

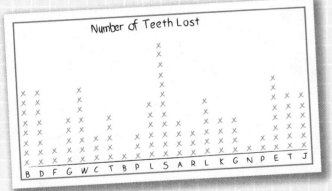

Henry's Work

On this type of *case-value graph,* each individual case or piece of data is shown separately as a quantity. The letters at the bottom are the first initials of the individual students. The column of **Xs** above each initial shows the number of teeth that each person lost. Starting at the left, Students B and D each lost 8 teeth, Student F lost 2 teeth, and so on. This graph is similar to the cube towers students created to show the pocket data.

Students may organize the data further by putting all of the cases with the same value next to each other as Holly does in her drawing of the cube towers she built.

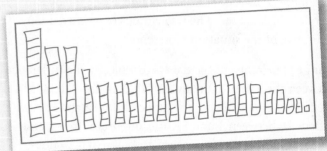

Holly's Work

In this representation, the value for each individual is shown clearly, and it is possible to see where there are many instances of the same value. For example, many students lost 5 teeth. It is also fairly easy to see the highest and lowest values. However, it is difficult to notice values that have no data or to describe where data are concentrated.

Other students make representations that group together all the data with the same value, showing each piece of data with a single symbol. For example, Leigh's representation from another classroom is shown below.

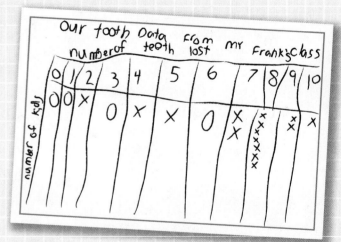

Leigh's Work

Leigh writes all of the values across the top of her representation and then uses **Xs** in the columns under each number—one **X** for each student who lost that number of teeth. She is using a representation that shows the *frequency distribution* of the data. It shows the frequency of occurrence of each value in the data set.

Like many students at this age, Leigh is not quite satisfied by using just an empty column to show that no students lost that number of teeth; she writes in 0 to indicate no students for that value. As she becomes more experienced in representing numerical data and sees more examples of others' representations, she will learn that an empty column can represent no data. You may refer to other examples so that students like Leigh can see that leaving a column blank is an acceptable way to represent no data.

Frequency distributions such as Leigh's clearly represent:

- The amount of data at each value

- Where data are concentrated

- Where there are few data

- The minimum and maximum values

- Whether there are any outliers

The columns of **Xs,** coupled with the numbers showing the values, provide an overall picture of how the data are spread.

In a case-value representation, each **X** or other symbol might represent a tooth, and a column of **Xs** might represent the number of teeth one person lost. In a frequency distribution such as Leigh's, one **X** represents one person. Its placement in a particular row or column indicates how many teeth that person lost. Students who use case-value representations and students who use frequency representations often have trouble understanding one another's representations. However, by comparing them, students learn a great deal about interpreting data representations.

Here is another example of a frequency distribution from a third classroom. Simon used a line plot to show how many people lost each number of teeth.

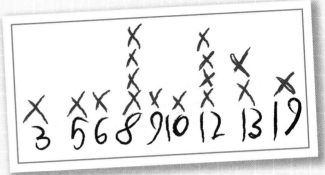

Simon's Work

In Simon's representation, only the values that have data are shown. No one lost 4, 7, 11, or 14–18 teeth, so these values are omitted on the scale of values. It is common for second graders to represent only values that occur in their data. Because they are focusing on the count of data at each individual value, they do not see any reason to include a value for which there are no data. With more experience in describing the data set as a whole, they begin to realize that leaving out values can obscure where data are concentrated and where there are gaps. As students compare representations, they begin to visualize how including values with no data reveals important information. In this case, the gap in the data from 13 to 19 is not visible in the representation.

In second grade, students gain experience with representations of frequency distributions such as line plots. Frequency distributions make the overall shape of numerical data more obvious—where data are concentrated, where there are few data, and how the data are spread from the minimum to the maximum values.

Although many students at this age primarily report the count of the data at each value—especially the value of the mode—they can also begin to notice aspects of the group as a whole. See **Dialogue Box:** Comparing Lost Teeth Data on page 142 for examples.

End-of-Unit Assessment

Problem 1: How Many Books in a Week?

This problem has two parts. In the first part, students represent the data collected from the students in their class about the number of books that they read in the past week. In the second part, students write what they noticed about the data.

Part 1: Ordering and Representing the Data

Benchmark addressed:

Benchmark 3: Order and represent a set of numerical data.

In order to meet the benchmark, students' work should show that they can:

- Order and accurately represent the class's responses to the question "How many books do you read in a week?"

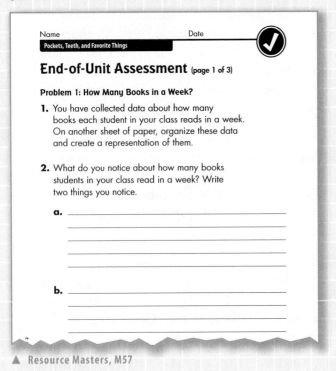

▲ Resource Masters, M57

Meeting the Benchmark

Students who meet the benchmark accurately order and represent the class data. They may represent their data in one of the following ways. Note that these samples are from two different second-grade classes, which accounts for the differences in the data sets.

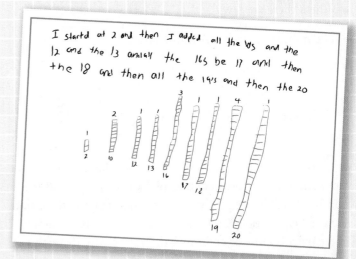

Katrina's Work

Alberto's Work

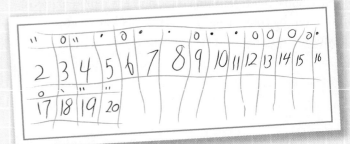

Rochelle's Work

Some students may create a line plot that leaves out the numbers for which there is no data. In later grades, students will be expected to include these numbers, but in this assessment, students were not asked to create a conventional line plot.

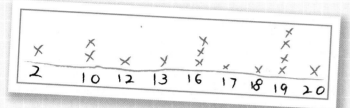

Anita's Work

Partially Meeting the Benchmark

Some students may represent and order the data clearly but they may misplace or fail to include some of the data in their representation. Ask these students to look carefully at their representations and to compare them with the data that they collected. Students who are able to find their mistakes meet the benchmark.

Not Meeting the Benchmark

Students who do not meet the benchmark may not order the data, but may instead represent the data in the order it has been collected.

Carla's Work

Students who do not meet the benchmark may show something that they learned about the data, but they may not order and represent the whole data set.

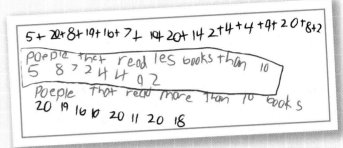

Darren's Work

Students who do not meet this benchmark will benefit from further opportunities to represent a set of numerical data.

Part 2: Describing the Data

Benchmark addressed:

Benchmark 4: Describe a numerical data set including the highest and lowest values and the mode.

In order to meet the benchmark, students' work should show that they can:

- Accurately describe, in 3 different statements, what the data show about the number of books students in their class read in a week.

Meeting the Benchmark

Students who meet the benchmark can write two different statements that describe the data. Students' descriptions of the data may include the following:

- The highest and lowest values—the greatest and the least number of books read in the class

- The mode—the most common number of books students read

- The number of students who read a given number of books

> the least number of books that people read is 2 and the hiyest is 20!

Roshaun's Work

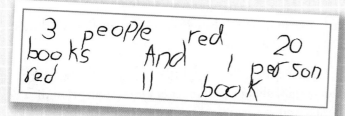

> 3 people red books red And red 20 11 book 1 person

Paige's Work

Partially Meeting the Benchmark

Some students may describe a data set accurately but may not relate it to what it shows about the number of books students read in a week.

> There are 3 20s. The lowist Number is 2 the Hiist is 20.

Chen's Work

Ask these students what their description shows about the number of books read in a week by students in the class. For example, say, "You said that there are three 20s. What do the 3 and the 20 stand for? What does that tell us about the number of books read in a week by students in this class?"

Not Meeting the Benchmark

Some students who do not meet the benchmark may make broad statements that do not refer to specific aspects of the data. For example, asking Juan to clarify what he means by "big numbers" may help him be more specific about the data he is describing.

> I notice that the Kids had read a lot of Books because I seen Big numbers.

Juan's Work

Some students who do not meet the benchmark may not describe the data or what it represents accurately. In this example, Malcolm comments on his individual piece of data.

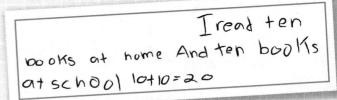

> I read ten books at home And ten books at school 10+10=20

Malcolm's Work

Some students may describe the data but may not focus on important aspects of the data.

> I noticed that four people was abset and the people who was abset all have "a" in there name.

Esteban's Work

All students who do not meet the benchmark can benefit from more opportunities to describe data sets. Some students may have difficulty gathering information from a representation or knowing what the data represent. Asking these students questions about what specific data points and values represent may help them to begin to gather information from representations. Others may have difficulty knowing what information to look for in a representation. Help these students by asking them to look for specific features of the data and by asking them to describe what these features show about the group surveyed.

Problem 2: Third Graders: How Many Books in a Week?

This problem has two parts. In the first part, students read and report the information they are able to gather from a representation of the number of books that a class of third graders read in a week. In the second part, students compare the number of books read in a week by students in their own class with the number of books read by students in the third-grade class.

Part 1: Reading a Data Representation

Students answer a series of questions about the number of books a class of third graders read in a week. This data is represented on a line plot.

Benchmark addressed:

Benchmark 5: Read and interpret a variety of representations of numerical and categorical data.

In order to meet the benchmark, students' work should show that they can:

- Accurately answer questions about a set of data represented in a line plot of the number of books third graders read in a week.

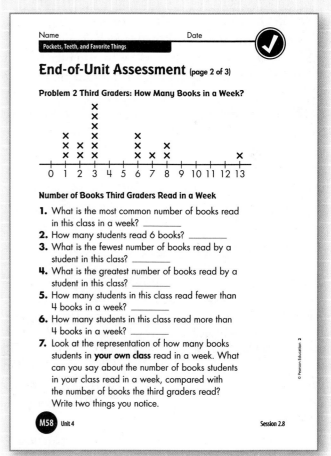

▲ Resource Masters, M58

Meeting the Benchmark

Students who meet the benchmark will respond correctly to Questions 1–6.

Partially Meeting the Benchmark

Students who partially meet the benchmark respond correctly to at least 3 of the 6 questions.

Some students who partially meet the benchmark may not have completely understood some of the questions asked. Ask the questions orally or reword the questions to determine whether students' difficulties were related to comprehension.

Other students, particularly those who have difficulty answering Questions 3 and 4, may not be completely sure whether the **Xs** in the line plot represent the number of books read or the number of people who read each quantity of books. Common incorrect answers for Question 3 are 7 and 13. A common incorrect answer for Question 4 is 3. These responses indicate that the student is interpreting the **X** on the line plot to mean the number of books read. In many cases, these same students will answer Questions 1 and 2 correctly. This is another indication that they are uncertain or only partially clear about what the **Xs** and/or numbers in the line plot represent.

Not Meeting the Benchmark

Students who do not meet the benchmark respond correctly to 2 or fewer questions. These students may not understand what the **Xs** or the numbers represent in the line plot.

Students who partially meet or do not meet the benchmark will benefit from seeing the same set of data represented in different ways, as with the pocket and teeth data. You may find that students are able to gather information from some representations and not from others. Making connections between a cube tower representation and a line plot will help students clarify what each aspect of the representation shows. In addition, asking students to read and find specific information in representations will also be helpful.

Part 2: Comparing Two Sets of Data

Benchmark addressed:

Benchmark 6: Compare two sets of numerical data.

In order to meet the benchmark, students' work should show that they can:

- Make two accurate comparisons between the number of books read in a week by students in their own class and the number of books read in a week by students in the third-grade class.

Meeting the Benchmark

Students' responses will vary, depending on what aspects of the data they compare. To meet the benchmark, students must compare the same aspect of the data in each classroom.

Students may compare the greatest or least number of books read in a week in each class. Leo also compares the total number of people in each classroom.

We have 20 for the highest and they have 13 for the highest. We have 16 in our class and they got 22.

Leo's Work

Students may compare the modes, or most common number of books read in each class.

One kid in 3rd grade read 13 book and some one read our class read 13 book. Three was the 3rd grade mode and our mode was 16 and 19.

Alberto's Work

Students may compare the number of students who read certain numbers of books.

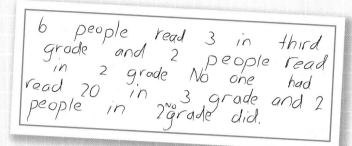

Yama's Work

Partially Meeting the Benchmark

Students who partially meet the benchmark may compare aspects of the data but may not relate the data to what they show about the comparison between their own class and the third-grade class. For example, a student might state, "In the third grade there are 2 on 2 and in our class there are 4 on 2."

Ask these students to explain what "2 on 2" and "4 on 2" mean, as well as how this comparison relates to the number of books read.

Making comparisons will be challenging for some second graders. Asking them to clarify their written statements may give you additional information about how students are thinking about the two sets of data. For example, although it is broad, Nate's statement may indicate that he is analyzing what the data from each class mean.

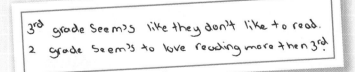

Nate's Work

Nate claims that the second graders like to read more than the third graders. One reason for his observation may be that the second graders read a greater number of books than the third graders. He ignores the possibility that books read by second graders have fewer pages, which would result in the second-grade class reading more books.

Not Meeting the Benchmark

Some students, such as Jeffrey, do not meet the benchmark because they describe the data inaccurately. Other students who do not meet the benchmark may describe aspects of the data accurately but may make no statements of comparison.

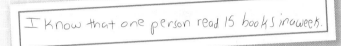

Jeffrey's Work

All students who do not meet the benchmark can benefit from more opportunities to compare sets of data. Some students may have difficulty reading and gathering information from a representation or knowing what the data represent. Others may have difficulty knowing what information to look for in a set of data. For some students, looking at two representations and finding similarities and differences may be challenging. It may help some students who have difficulty comparing two sets of data first to describe the data in one set and then to compare the specific features they describe with similar features in the other set.

Problem 3: Guess My Rule with Names

In this problem, students choose two rules to sort a set of names. Students write down their rules, and then sort the names using a Venn diagram.

Benchmarks addressed:

Benchmark 1: Use a Venn diagram to sort data by two attributes.

Benchmark 2: Identify categories for a set of categorical data and organize the data into the chosen categories.

In order to meet the benchmarks, students' work should show that they can:

- Choose and record two rules that fit some of the attributes of the names;

- Sort the names accurately in the Venn diagram, according to the two chosen rules.

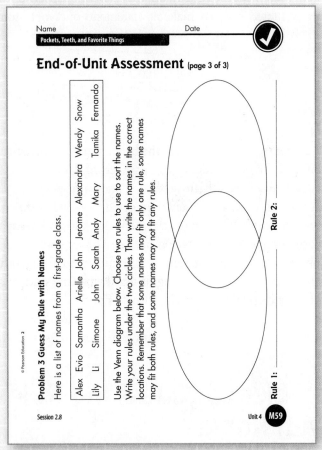

▲ Resource Masters, M59

Meeting the Benchmark

Look for the following criteria in students' solutions:

- Students have identified two rules that fit the attributes of some of the names;

- Based on the rules that they chose students have placed all of the names in the correct circle, in the overlap of the two circles, or outside the circles.

Possible rules that students may identify include these:

- Names that contain a certain letter

- Names starting or ending with certain letters

- Names that contain a certain number of letters

- Names that are considered boys' or girls' names

Some combinations of rules will lead to no names in the overlap of the circles.

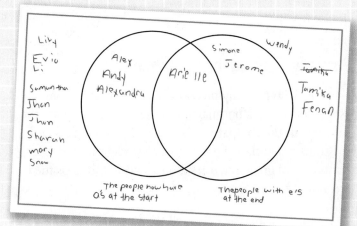

Carolina's Work

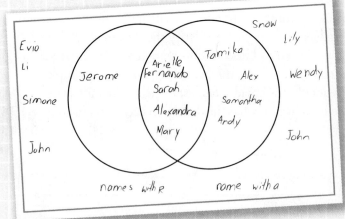

Yama's Work

Partially Meeting the Benchmark

Students may identify two rules that fit the attributes of some, but not all, of the names. Although Juanita sorted all the names that fit her two rules correctly, she did not include on her representation the names that did not fit her rules.

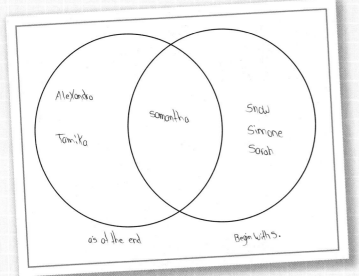

Juanita's Work

Students may also misplace some of the names. For example, Melissa misplaced the names Fernando and Wendy.

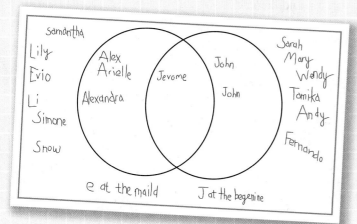

Melissa's Work

Some students will have had difficulty sorting or using a Venn diagram, but others may simply have made an accidental error. Ask students to check whether they have sorted all the names correctly according to the rules they chose. If they correct their mistakes, they have met the benchmark.

If students do not correct their mistakes, they may need additional support for sorting by attributes. These students may be able to identify appropriate rules but may not yet understand how to sort the objects by their chosen rules.

Not Meeting the Benchmarks

Students who do not meet the benchmark may have difficulty choosing and specifying a rule or rules to sort the data.

A few students may not place any names that fit both rules in the overlap of the two circles. This may indicate that they do not understand how a piece of data can fit two rules, or that they do not understand how to use a Venn diagram to represent data that fit two rules.

A few students may not be able to choose appropriate rules or sort any of the names according to the rules they chose. These students may not understand how to identify common attributes or how to sort by attributes.

In the following examples, both students selected a letter to sort the names but were not specific about using the letter. They also did not include all of the data in the Venn diagram.

In Monisha's work, neither rule is specific. We might assume that Rule 1 is supposed to be "Names that begin with J," judging by the placement of John, John, and Jerome. However, because Rule 2 is not specific and because only 1 name appears, the intended rule could have been any of the following:

- Names that end in *e*

- Names that contain the letter *e*

- Names with 2 *e*'s

Although the name *Jerome* is placed correctly, there are other names in the data set—Simone, Arielle, Alex, Evio, Alexandra, Wendy, and Fernando—that could also have been included in the right-hand circle. When Monisha's teacher asked her to clarify her thinking, she had difficulty explaining Rule 2 and choosing other names to include.

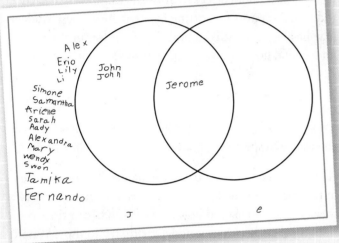

Monisha's Work

In Henry's case, the rules are not specific. In addition, there are other names—Lily, Wendy, and Andy—that end in or contain the letter *y* that should have been included in the Venn diagram. Henry also did not account for the names that did not fit either rule.

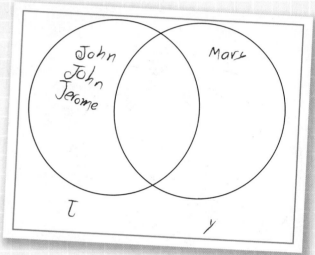

Henry's Work

All students, particularly those who do not meet the benchmark, will benefit from continued opportunities to sort, categorize, and represent in a Venn diagram data with overlapping attributes. Consider how you might use Venn diagrams in other subject areas such as science, social studies, and literacy.

This Yektti Fits in Both Groups

This activity is an introduction to *Guess My Rule* with Yekttis with Two Rules. The class is gathered around a sheet of chart paper. On the paper are two non-overlapping circles.

Teacher: Yesterday, we played *Guess My Rule* with Yekttis. Today, we are going to play again, but a little differently. I am going to use my word cards that describe the attributes of the Yekttis, except today, I am going to put one card here (point to one circle) and one here (point to the other circle). I have two secret rules today.

We talked yesterday about the different attributes of the Yekttis—their shapes, antennae, and eyes—and how some of them were the same and some were different. You will use all that information today to help you play this game.

The teacher places a word card face down in each circle. She puts two Yektti Cards in one circle, two Yektti Cards in the other circle, and two Yektti Cards outside the circles.

Leo places a hexagon Yektti with 3 antennae and open eyes outside both circles.

Teacher: Yes, that is where it belongs. Good. The ones that don't fit in the groups will help you figure out the ones that do.

Holly: Does this one fit?

Holly holds up a hexagon with 1 antenna and closed eyes.

Teacher: Actually, it doesn't fit either of my rules. That gives us more important information.

Young puts a hexagon Yektti with 4 antennae and opened eyes in one circle.

Teacher: Young, it actually goes here, in this group.

Leigh: Does this one fit this rule?

Leigh puts a triangle Yektti with 3 antennae and closed eyes in the circle with the other triangle Yekttis.

Teacher: Yes, it does. I think you might be starting to figure this one out.

Henry holds up a triangle Yektti with 4 antennae and solid eyes.

Teacher: Where do you think that one goes?

Henry shrugs.

Carla: It could go in both groups.

Amaya: Put it in the middle.

Teacher: Amaya says to put it in the middle. Let's try that.

Henry puts the card in between the two circles. Then the class sorts a few more cards.

Teacher: Who thinks he or she knows the rule in this group? (Point to the triangle-rule circle.)

Class: Triangles!

Teacher: Let's see. (Turn over the word card.) That's right!

The students guess correctly that the other rule is 4 antennae.

Teacher: So all of these were triangles and all of these had 4 antennae. But wait, why did Amaya say to put this one in the middle?

Anita: There's another just like it but with wide eyes.

Anita picks up a triangle Yektti with 4 antennae and open eyes.

Teacher: Does it fit in this group, and this group? Let's take Amaya's idea and put it here in the middle.

Carla: You could take both circles and put them together in the middle.

Teacher: Hold on to that idea for a minute, Carla. Let's look at these groups again. What is this group?

Class: Triangles!

Teacher: And this group?

Class: 4 antennae!

Teacher: And how about the ones in the middle?

Class: Similar . . . , the same . . . , half 4 antennas/half triangle . . . , it's medium.

Teacher: The ones in the middle have 4 antennae and are triangles. Carla suggested taking the circles and putting them together in the middle.

The teacher takes out a Venn diagram drawn on chart paper.

Teacher: Is this what you were thinking? This is a called a Venn diagram. Mathematicians use it when things fit in more than one group. The middle section is part of the circle on the left and part of the circle on the right. So, let's put the cards from this game on here. Who can find the cards that go just in the triangle group? In the 4 antennae group? And how about the middle group?

The students sort all the cards.

Carla: There's only one thing different about those in the middle—just eyes. But we were only talking about antennae and triangles.

At the beginning of this activity, the teacher helps students focus on gathering information from the Yekttis that have been sorted, emphasizing the information that can be gained from the Yekttis that do not fit either rule. The students soon are faced with a problem: What do we do with Yekttis that fit both rules? The teacher uses students' ideas of how to organize the Yekttis that fit both rules as an introduction to the Venn diagram. The teacher asks students to continue sorting the cards by using the Venn diagram, helping students remember how to use each area.

What's Your Favorite Weekend Activity?

Students have been organizing the "Favorite Weekend Activity" data that they collected in Session 1.2 in different ways. During this session, students organize this set of data one more way and then, as a group, discuss what they have learned.

Teacher: We are going to organize our favorite weekend activity data in one more way. Someone suggested that one category could be sports. Do you see any of your responses that could fit in a sports category?

Students point out 4 different responses that could fit under sports.

Teacher: If *sports* is one of our categories, what other categories could there be? Last time we used *inside and outside activities.* What other categories would go along with sports? We could have a few different categories, not just two.

Gregory: Alone activities?

Teacher: We could say *alone activities,* but let's see whether we can think of some other ones that really fit with sports. So, we have some activities that are sports activities. What other kinds of activities do we have?

Luis: Some people like to do art things, like drawing or making things.

Teacher: Art is a good category.

The teacher writes *Sports* and *Art* on stick-on notes and moves the activities students suggest under these categories.

Teacher: Look at the activities that are left. What are some categories they can fit in that go with sports and art?

Tia: How about games? People said they liked things like video games and playing cards and stuff like that.

The teacher writes *Games* and moves *video games* and *playing cards* under that category.

Darren: But baseball and soccer are games, too. Wouldn't they go there?

Teacher: What do you think, should we put baseball and soccer in between sports and games, like we did with activities that were done both indoors and outdoors?

Nadia: But they're different. In soccer and baseball you run around. With video games and cards you just sit.

Lonzell: Maybe we could call them *sitting games.*

Other students nod their heads. The teacher writes *Sitting* above *Games* on the stick-on note.

Juan: Reading would be good. Some people said reading, or reading with Mom, or going to the library. Let's do reading.

The teacher writes *Reading* on a stick-on note and moves the reading activities that students suggest under it.

Teacher: So what do we have left?

Tia: Two TVs, one eating, one go to the science museum, one play on the playground.

Teacher: What category or categories could we put those in?

Luis: They don't really go together. They're all different. I can't think of one.

Juan: Can't we just say leftovers?

Teacher: Sometimes people make a category called *Other* for things that don't really fit into any of the groups. Maybe we could do that with these. So what can we say about the favorite weekend activities of students in this class, given the way we organized the data this time?

Rochelle: More people like to do sports than anything else.

Monisha: But not a lot more, just two people more than *Other* and *Art,* which had a tie.

Nate: But *Other* doesn't count because it's not really a category. They don't go together.

Nadia: People like to do lots of different kinds of things, but most of all, sports.

Teacher: We organized our data in a few different ways—by outdoor and indoor activities; by activities you do alone, with friends, or with family; and by sports, art, reading, sitting games, and other. Who can tell us what we learned about the favorite activities of students in this class from looking at these different ways of organizing this data?

Simon: People like to do outdoor things, sports, and activities with friends.

Carla: They like to do both outdoor and indoor things, activities with friends and family, and all different kinds of activities, but more people's favorites are outdoor activities, sports, and activities with friends.

Teacher: So even though we just had the same data each time, we learned different things about people's favorite activities, depending on how we organized the data and what categories we put it in.

The students in this class work together to decide on categories to use to sort their Favorite Weekend Activity data. During their discussion they choose categories that "go together," decide what to do with data that seem to fit more than one category, and decide what to do with data that do not seem to fit any categories. Working on these issues will help students later on when they sort their own "Favorite Things" survey data.

Describing Pocket Data

Students have been working in small groups to organize towers of cubes in different ways. These towers represent the number of pockets each student in the class is wearing. In this discussion, the teacher asks students to gather information from the pocket-tower representation and talk about what this information tells them about the number of pockets each student is wearing.

Teacher: Who would like to arrange these pocket towers? Who can organize them in a way that tells us something about the number of pockets people are wearing today?

Amaya: I'm going to try to find doubles. (Amaya puts towers with the same height next to each other.)

Teacher: So you're putting towers next to each other that have the same number.

Amaya: And I'm going to organize them like Chen did, from the tallest to the shortest.

Teacher: Let's take a look at this. What can we tell from looking at the towers about the number of pockets that people are wearing today?

Darren: I see that some numbers are the same. These all have partners but this one doesn't (points to the tower of 3; there is only 1 tower of 3).

Henry: There are two 2s.

Melissa: There are lots of 5s.

Teacher: You said that there are lots of 5s. What does one of these towers of 5 cubes tell us?

Monisha: That's how much 1 kid was wearing.

Teacher: How many pockets was this student wearing (points to tower of 5 cubes)?

Monisha: Five.

Teacher: Is there somewhere else in our data where you can find another person with 5 pockets?

Roshaun points to the 4 other cube towers of 5.

Teacher: What did Roshaun just find?

Amaya: Five 5s.

Carolina: Five people with 5 pockets.

Teacher: So what else can you say about the number of pockets people are wearing?

Henry: Two people are wearing 2 pockets.

Esteban: Nobody is wearing 7 pockets.

Teacher: Are there any other numbers of pockets that nobody is wearing?

Esteban: One pocket.

Teacher: How many pocket towers do we have in this representation?

Monisha: 17.

Teacher: What's missing? Think about how many people are in this class.

Roshaun: The people who had 0 pockets.

Teacher: How many people had 0 pockets? How can we show that?

Roshaun: 3.

The students write 0 on 3 self-stick notes for the 3 people with 0 pockets.

Teacher: What is the greatest number of pockets that people had? Melissa, where can you find the most number of pockets? (Melissa is not sure.) Luis, do you know?

Luis: The last one (points to the towers of 8 cubes).

Teacher: What does this part tell us?

Roshaun: Who has the most pockets?

Melissa: Three people.

Teacher: These represent 3 people. And how many pockets did these 3 people have?

Melissa: 8.

Teacher: Where are the people who had the least number of pockets?

Malcolm points to 3 self-stick notes with 0 on them.

Teacher: So, the number of pockets in this class ranges from 0 to 8. When I look at this representation, where can I see a whole bunch of people that have the same number of pockets?

Carla points to the towers of 5 cubes.

Teacher: So this group here had the most common number of pockets (points to the towers of 5 cubes). How many pockets did each of these people have?

Anita: 5. And that's 25.

Teacher: What does that 25 represent?

Anita: 25 pockets.

Teacher: I'm going to teach you a word that you'll learn more about in Grade 3. That word is *mode*. This group here has the most common number of pockets. That's called the *mode*.

At the beginning of this discussion, students find towers with the same quantity of cubes but do not connect those quantities to the number of pockets students are wearing. The teacher quickly focuses the students on this connection by asking the students what a specific tower represents. The teacher continues to guide the students in describing specific aspects of the data, including the greatest number of pockets, the least number of pockets, the mode, and values for which there is no data. Through this discussion, the teacher asks students to find important features of the data in the representation and to connect the features to the number of pockets and the number of people.

Dialogue Box

Collecting Data from Other Classrooms

Students in this class are preparing to collect data from other classrooms. Before they go, they recount their feelings of nervousness about this project and discuss how to get help from classroom teachers and from other students.

Nadia: Do the teachers know we're coming?

Teacher: Yes, they know that you're coming, and most of the teachers have told their students.

Simon: We're going to use the class lists to check everyone off. But what if we can't read the names on the class list?

Juan: You could ask a kid in the classroom. Or you could ask a teacher; that's what teachers are there for.

Teacher: Those are good suggestions.

Jeffrey: What if you're sort of embarrassed? I don't think I'd be embarrassed if I was going to a first-grade classroom, but I'm going to a fourth-grade classroom.

Teacher: Any ideas about what to do?

Rochelle: I'd try to look for someone in the class that I know.

Jeffrey: But what if you're embarrassed and what if someone laughs?

Teacher: The teacher in the classroom is there to help you collect the data. Going into a classroom of older students is not an easy thing for some people to do. Jeffrey, how about if I walk down to your classroom with you and your partner and stay around until you get started?

Katrina: Well, in our group, Travis said that he doesn't talk to people he doesn't know. So we decided that he can check off the names and write down the numbers and I'll ask the questions.

After students return from collecting their data, the teacher asks students to reflect on the process.

Teacher: Before you left, some of you talked about how you felt about going into other classrooms. How did it go?

Carla: It was much easier than I thought it would be, but I was a little embarrassed.

Rochelle: I was a tiny bit scared.

Henry: I got a little nervous because we knocked on the door twice and the teacher didn't hear us, so we just had to open the door and we couldn't say "excuse me" because the teacher was talking. And finally the teacher saw us.

Carolina: I thought it was exciting and very fun!

Roshaun: I was kind of surprised because I was expecting that people would have high numbers because we were in a fourth grade class. I was surprised that some students had lost fewer teeth than some second graders.

Juanita: I thought most kids in Kindergarten would have lost 2 or 3 or 4 teeth, but it wasn't that way. Lots of kids lost only 1.

Leigh: I was surprised that in fourth grade only 1 person lost 6 teeth and 1 person said that he lost 16. That surprised me because that's a lot of teeth.

Monisha: We went to the Kindergarten class, and we thought the numbers would be 0, 1, and 2, and they were!

Collecting data is an important aspect of the data analysis process. However, data collection can be challenging for teachers and often scary for second graders. Discussing their nervousness before going to the classes allowed students to express their concerns and do some problem solving. The discussion afterward gave students the opportunity to reflect on the process. The discussion naturally shifted from how the students were feeling about collecting the data, to comparing their predictions, to what they actually found out when they collected the data.

Comparing Lost Teeth Data

Students have collected data from other classes about the number of teeth students have lost. They are looking at their representations and comparing the other classes' data with the data for their own class. Representations from Kindergarten and Grades 1, 3, 4, and 5 are posted. The teacher asked the students who worked on Kindergarten representations to report what they noticed first.

Leo: In Kindergarten, the range was 0 to 6, and there were a lot of people who lost 0 teeth.

Teacher: How many of them lost 0 teeth?

Rochelle: Ten people lost 0 teeth and there are 21 kids in the class. So that's around half.

Teacher: So close to half of the Kindergarten class lost 0 teeth.

Leo: But there was 1 kid who lost 7 and that's the same as in our class.

Teacher: You're noticing that 1 kindergartner lost 7 teeth and that there's also 1 person in our class who lost 7 teeth. That's one way the Kindergarten class is similar to our class. Are there other ways that the Kindergarten class is the same as our class or different from our class? What can the rest of you notice from Leo's and Rochelle's representation?

Henry: For the Kindergarten class, that's the top of the list, and for our class, that's at the bottom.

Teacher: What do you mean by "top of the list"? Does someone else know what Henry is saying?

Monisha: Yes, their highest is 7, but 7 is one of our lowest.

Juan: Actually, I think they're really different because they're clumping around 0, 1, and 2, and we're clumping around 8 and 9.

Teacher: Juan is saying that in the Kindergarten class, there's a clump here at 0, 1, and 2, and in our class there's a clump at 8 and 9. What does that tell us about the number of teeth the kindergartners lost, compared with the number of teeth our class lost?

Young: Most of the kindergarteners lost 0 or 1 or 2 teeth, but most of us lost 8 or 9.

Teacher: Is Young right? Did most of the kindergartners lose 0 or 1 or 2 teeth?

Lonzell: Yes, because if you count them up, it's 10 and 3 and 4. That's 17. That's almost all of the Kindergarten kids.

Teacher: What about one of the other grades? Is there another one that you think is different from our class?

Holly: We were surprised that 1 first grader lost 13 teeth because our highest was 12, and we're a year older.

Alberto: Some kids might lose their teeth when they're younger. My brother's 5, and he already lost a lot of teeth.

Jeffrey: I lost my first 3 teeth when I was 4. So maybe some kids start early.

Carolina: Maybe some of those teeth had to get pulled.

Teacher: You're seeing one thing about the first-grade class—that they had one person with a higher number of lost teeth than you expected. But what about the rest of the first grade? In general, how does the first-grade class compare with our class?

Malcolm: There was 1 boy who didn't lose any teeth, but he was young for his grade.

Esteban: Their big clump is lower. It's mostly here, between 2 and 5. It's pushed down from our clump.

Melissa: The 2, 3, 4, and 5 are all squished together.

Teacher: What does that tell us about our class, compared with the first-grade class? Who can say something using the word *teeth* and not just numbers?

Anita: We're a little higher in lost teeth because we're a little older.

Chen: Most of them lost 2, 3, 4, or 5 teeth, but most of us lost 7 or 8 teeth.

Nadia: We've had another year to lose teeth.

Comparing and contrasting different groups often yields better descriptions of the data. By contrasting 2 or more groups, students may be more likely to notice where data are concentrated and where there are few data.

In this conversation, students notice that there is 1 unusually high value in the first-grade data. The piece of data that shows that 1 first grader lost more teeth than any of them is interesting to students, and they begin to speculate about why this value might exist. However, the teacher also wants students to notice that overall, the first-grade class lost fewer total teeth. So, she steers the conversation back to the overall shape of the first-grade data.

Discussing Mystery Data

Before this discussion, students tried to determine which set of mystery data (Class A, B, C, or D) another student in the class represented in a line plot. They are now discussing how they determined each set.

Teacher: If you think you had a line plot that represented the data from Class A, can you share how you made that decision?

Travis: First, I checked to see whether there was a 14 on the line plot, and then I kept going down the list.

Teacher: What do you mean by "went down the list"?

Travis: I looked at each list and then I saw that my graph had one 14 and two 11s. So, I found the classroom that had one 14 and two 11s and I checked all the numbers.

Teacher: So you tried to match a piece of data on your line plot to one of the lists?

Travis: Yes.

Tamara: I noticed that my line plot had lots of people who had lost 8 teeth, so I looked for that clue.

Leigh: There weren't any small numbers on my line plot, so I knew it couldn't be Class B or C.

Teacher: It's interesting that you all used a similar strategy. First, you looked for something interesting about your representation. Then, you used that information to look at all of the sets of Mystery Teeth Data. How about Class B?

Simon: It's easy. The numbers went from 1 tooth to 13 teeth, I just looked for data that had 1 to 13 teeth, and that was B.

Holly: I kind of did the same thing. It was easy because there weren't many different numbers, and they didn't go up very high.

Teacher: Can you explain what you mean by that?

Holly: The teeth that were lost went from 0 to 4. And I think I know which grade Class C is collected from.

Teacher: How many of you think you know what grade Class C represents? Tell someone nearby what you think and why.

Travis (to Holly): It's Kindergarten. It practically matches the data that we collected from our Kindergarten rooms. In first grade, lots of kids lose 3 to 5 teeth, and some lose more, so I don't think Class C is a first-grade class.

Holly: I agree.

Teacher: As you were talking to your partner, I heard some of you mention the small range of numbers. Some of you also talked about comparing the data to the data we collected.

Jeffrey: You know what was confusing? The line plot I had went from 5 to 14 teeth, but then I noticed that two of the classes had that same thing— Classes A and D. I couldn't just use the most and the least number of teeth.

Teacher: So what other information did you use?

Jeffrey: Paul showed me that Class D didn't have very many kids in it. I counted the kids on the line plot I had and there was 1 less kid than on D. I think the person forgot to put someone's teeth on the line plot, but I still think it's D.

Teacher: A few people said that their graphs had some mistakes. Can you politely point out the differences you noticed between the line plot and the set of data?

Students used a variety of strategies to match representations to the Mystery Teeth Data. Some students looked for important features of the data, such as the most common number of teeth lost. Others considered the range from lowest value to highest value in both the line plot and the mystery data sets. The teacher helped students see the similarities and differences between the strategies by generalizing the strategies that students shared. Students in this class found comparing important features of the data a useful tool for matching the line plots to the lists of mystery data.

The *Student Math Handbook* pages related to this unit are pictured on the following pages. This book is designed to be used flexibly: as a resource for students doing classwork, as a book students can take home for reference while doing homework and playing math games with their families, and as a reference for families to better understand the work their children are doing in class.

When students take the *Student Math Handbook* home, they and their families can discuss these pages together to reinforce or enhance students' understanding of the mathematical concepts and games in this unit.

Math Words and Ideas

Plus 10 Combinations

Any single-digit number plus 10 is a Plus 10 combination. So is 10 plus any single-digit number. Here are all of the Plus 10 combinations you are working on.

10 + 0 = 10	
0 + 10 = 10	
10 + 1 = 11	
1 + 10 = 11	
10 + 2 = 12	
2 + 10 = 12	
10 + 3 = 13	
3 + 10 = 13	
10 + 4 = 14	
4 + 10 = 14	
10 + 5 = 15	
5 + 10 = 15	
10 + 6 = 16	
6 + 10 = 16	
10 + 7 = 17	
7 + 10 = 17	
10 + 8 = 18	
8 + 10 = 18	
10 + 9 = 19	
9 + 10 = 19	

? What patterns do you notice in the Plus 10 combinations? Which ones do you know? Which are you still working on?

fifty-one **SMH 51**

Math Words and Ideas, p. 51

Math Words and Ideas

Data

Math Words
• data

The information you collect is called data. One way to collect data is by asking a group of people the same question.

For example, Ms. Williams was planning an after-school program for second graders. She started by collecting data.

Ms. Williams collected the data to find out what second graders like to do after school.

Here is Ms. Williams's question.

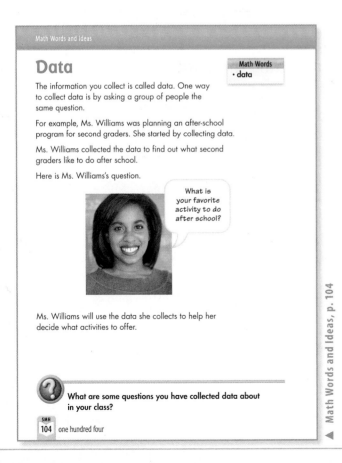

What is your favorite activity to do after school?

Ms. Williams will use the data she collects to help her decide what activities to offer.

? What are some questions you have collected data about in your class?

SMH 104 one hundred four

Math Words and Ideas, p. 104

Math Words and Ideas

Survey

Math Words
• survey

Doing a survey is a way to collect data. You conduct a survey by asking a group of people the same question and keeping track of their answers.

Here is Ms. Williams's after-school survey with the answers given by students.

What is your favorite activity to do after school?			
Student	Favorite Activity	Student	Favorite Activity
Alberto	Draw	Jacy	Play soccer
Anita	Check out books	Leigh	Play the piano
Carla	Play tag	Leo	Go to the playground
Carolina	Paint	Nate	Sew
Chen	Read stories and act out plays	Malcolm	Draw
Esteban	Listen to music	Gregory	Pretend
Henry	Play sports	Rochelle	Read stories and make up puppet shows
Holly	Dress up and act out plays	Simon	Play the drums
Jeffrey	T-ball	Yama	Go to the playground

one hundred five **SMH 105**

Math Words and Ideas, p. 105

Making Categories (page 1 of 2)

Putting data into categories can help you learn something about the group you surveyed.

Ms. Williams got many different responses from the students. She put them into categories to figure out which after-school classes to offer.

After looking at the data closely, Ms. Williams noticed that many of the students liked to do art activities. She decided to make one after-school class for these students.

ART CLASS	
Student	**Favorite Activity**
Alberto	Draw
Carolina	Paint
Nate	Sew
Malcolm	Draw

Look at the data on page 105.
What other categories could Ms. Williams make?
What other classes should be held?

▲ Math Words and Ideas, p. 106

Making Categories (page 2 of 2)

Ms. Williams looked at all the students' answers and put similar answers together. Making categories helped her figure out which after-school classes were needed.

Here are the categories.

Kind of Class	Students' Answers
Art	Draw, paint, sew, draw
Sports and outdoor play	Play tag, play sports, T-ball, play soccer, go to the playground, go to the playground
Pretend play	Pretend, dress up and act out plays, read stories and make up puppet shows
Music	Listen to music, play the piano, play the drums
Library	Check out books, read stories and act out plays, dress up and act out plays, read stories and make up puppet shows

Some of the answers in Pretend play and Library are the same.

What activities appear in both Pretend play and Library?

▲ Math Words and Ideas, p. 107

Venn Diagrams

Math Words
• Venn diagram

Ms. Williams thought the students would be happy with the classes, but there was a problem. There were 5 classes, but only 4 teachers. What could she do?

Ms. Williams looked at the data again. She noticed that some of the activities were very similar. Students in the Pretend play category liked to read stories and act out plays, and so did students in the Library category. She made a Venn diagram to help her think about this.

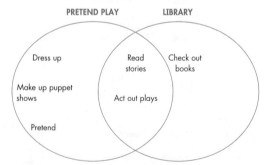

Looking at the Venn diagram helped Ms. Williams see that there was some overlap between the two classes. She decided to join the classes so that all the students in Pretend play and Library could read and act out stories and plays. The new after-school class was called Drama.

▲ Math Words and Ideas, p. 108

Organizing the Data

It was time for Ms. Williams to figure out which rooms to use. There were some big rooms and some small rooms. She needed to figure out which after-school classes had the most students in them and which classes were smaller.

 Can you think of a way to help Ms. Williams organize her data?

Ms. Williams looked at her data again and made this graph.

Art	Music	Sports and Outdoor Play	Drama
		Yama	
		Leo	Gregory
Malcolm		Jacy	Rochelle
Nate	Simon	Jeffrey	Holly
Carolina	Leigh	Henry	Chen
Alberto	Esteban	Carla	Anita

Which class will need the largest space?
How many more children are in Art than in Music?
How many children will be in the after-school classes altogether?

▲ Math Words and Ideas, p. 109

A Line Plot

Math Words
• line plot

In school, you will collect data about how many pockets all the students in your class are wearing. You can represent the data on a line plot. Here is an example from one second-grade class.

How Many Pockets Are You Wearing?

Each **X** stands for one student.

These numbers show the number of pockets.

Three students are wearing 0 pockets.
One student is wearing 1 pocket.
One student is wearing 2 pockets.

How many students are wearing 4 pockets?
How many students are wearing 8 pockets?
How many students answered the question?
What else do you notice?

SMH 110 one hundred ten

▲ Math Words and Ideas, p. 110

Talking About Data

Math Words
• highest value
• lowest value
• range
• mode
• outlier

Here is the same graph about pockets. Take another look.

How Many Pockets Are You Wearing?

There are many words that you can use to talk about data with numbers. Here are some of them.

Word	How It is Used in This Graph
highest value	11 pockets is the greatest number of pockets that a child in this class is wearing.
lowest value	0 pockets is the fewest number of pockets that a child in this class is wearing.
range	The number of pockets ranges from 0 to 11 in this class.
mode	The most common number of pockets is 4.
outlier	11 pockets is the outlier in this class. This is an unusual number of pockets.

one hundred eleven **111 SMH**

▲ Math Words and Ideas, p. 111

Index

IN THIS UNIT